MICROSOFT ONEDRIVE GUIDE 2024 FOR BEGINNERS

AWEISA MOSERAYA

INTRODUCTION

In the digital age, the way we store, access, and manage information has undergone a radical transformation. Gone are the days when physical storage devices were the only means to keep our important documents, photos, and files. Cloud storage has emerged as a revolutionary technology, offering unparalleled convenience, security, and accessibility. Among the myriad of cloud storage solutions available today, Microsoft OneDrive stands out as a robust and versatile option, catering to the needs of individuals, professionals, and enterprises alike.

Welcome to the "Microsoft OneDrive Guide 2024 for Beginners," your comprehensive resource for mastering OneDrive. Whether you are new to cloud storage or looking to optimize your use of OneDrive, this guide is designed to provide you with the knowledge and tools you need to leverage this powerful platform to its fullest potential. From setting up your OneDrive account to exploring advanced features, this book covers every aspect of OneDrive in a clear, step-by-step manner.

The Evolution of OneDrive

OneDrive has come a long way since its inception. Launched initially as Windows Live Folders in 2007, and later rebranded as SkyDrive, OneDrive has evolved significantly, adapting to the changing needs of users and the advancements in technology. Today, OneDrive is not just a storage solution; it is an integral part of the Microsoft ecosystem, seamlessly integrated with Office applications, Teams, SharePoint, and more.

The journey of OneDrive from a simple file storage service to a comprehensive cloud solution is a testament to Microsoft's commitment to innovation and user satisfaction. This evolution has been driven by a deep understanding of user needs and a relentless pursuit of excellence. With each update and enhancement, OneDrive has become more intuitive, more secure, and more powerful.

Why Choose OneDrive?

Choosing the right cloud storage solution is crucial, and OneDrive offers several compelling reasons to be your go-to choice:

1. **Integration with Microsoft 365**: OneDrive's seamless integration with Microsoft 365 (formerly Office 365) is a significant advantage. Whether you are using Word, Excel, PowerPoint, or Outlook, OneDrive ensures that your documents are easily accessible and shareable across all these platforms.

2. **Accessibility**: OneDrive allows you to access your files from any device with an internet connection. Whether you are working from your desktop at home, your laptop at the office, or your mobile device on the go, OneDrive ensures that your files are always within reach.

3. **Collaboration**: In today's interconnected world, collaboration is key. OneDrive's real-time co-authoring features allow multiple users to work on the same document simultaneously, making it an ideal tool for team projects and remote work.

4. **Security**: Security is a top priority for OneDrive. With features like two-step verification, encryption, and ransomware detection, OneDrive provides a secure environment for your data.

5. **Versatility**: OneDrive is not just for storing documents. It supports a wide range of file types, including photos, videos, and PDFs, and offers tools for file organization, sharing, and backup.

The OneDrive Mindset

Adopting OneDrive means more than just using a new tool; it involves embracing a new way of managing your digital life. The OneDrive mindset is about leveraging the cloud to enhance productivity, ensure data security, and foster collaboration. It's about understanding the potential of cloud storage to simplify your workflows and streamline your tasks.

This guide will help you adopt the OneDrive mindset, showing you how to integrate OneDrive into your daily routines and maximize its benefits. Whether you are an individual looking to organize your personal files, a student needing tools for academic work, or a business professional aiming to enhance productivity, this book will provide you with practical insights and tips.

A Comprehensive Guide

This book is structured to take you from the basics of OneDrive to its most advanced features. It begins with an introduction to OneDrive, covering its history, development, and the benefits of using this cloud storage service. From there, you will learn about setting up your OneDrive account, syncing your files, and managing your storage efficiently.

The guide also delves into the competitive landscape, comparing OneDrive with other cloud storage solutions to help you understand its unique advantages. You will discover how to ensure security and privacy for your data, explore advanced features, and learn strategies for backup and recovery.

To enhance your OneDrive experience, the book offers tips and tricks that can save you time and improve your productivity. It also addresses common problems users might encounter and provides practical solutions. Finally, you will explore real-world applications of OneDrive, demonstrating how this tool can be used effectively in various scenarios.

Your Journey with OneDrive

Embarking on your journey with OneDrive will open up new possibilities for how you manage and interact with your digital content. This guide is designed to be your companion, providing clear instructions, helpful tips, and valuable insights every step of the way. By the end of this book, you will have a thorough understanding of OneDrive and the confidence to use it to its full potential.

Whether you are just getting started with cloud storage or looking to deepen your knowledge, the "Microsoft OneDrive Guide 2024 for Beginners" is here to support you. The digital world is constantly evolving, and staying updated with the latest tools and technologies is essential. OneDrive is a powerful ally in this journey, offering a reliable and versatile platform for all your storage needs.

As you progress through this book, take the time to explore and experiment with OneDrive's features. The more you engage with the platform, the more proficient you will become. Cloud storage is not just a technological advancement; it is a shift in how we think about data, work, and collaboration. Embracing this shift will empower you to work smarter, stay organized, and achieve more.

Conclusion

The "Microsoft OneDrive Guide 2024 for Beginners" is more than just a manual; it is a gateway to a new way of managing your digital life. By understanding the principles and practices outlined in this guide, you will be well-equipped to harness the full power of OneDrive. From basic file storage to advanced collaboration tools, OneDrive offers a wealth of features designed to enhance your productivity and streamline your workflows.

As you delve into the chapters of this book, you will gain a deeper appreciation for the capabilities of OneDrive. Each section is crafted to provide you with practical knowledge and actionable steps, ensuring that you can apply what you learn immediately. The goal is to make your experience with OneDrive as smooth and rewarding as possible.

In today's fast-paced digital landscape, having a reliable and efficient cloud storage solution is indispensable. OneDrive stands out as a leader in this field, offering a blend of accessibility, security, and versatility that is hard to match. This guide is your key to unlocking the potential of OneDrive, transforming how you store, access, and share your files.

Welcome to the world of OneDrive. Let this guide be your roadmap as you navigate the features, tools, and possibilities that OneDrive has to offer. Whether you are a novice user or someone looking to refine your skills, the "Microsoft OneDrive Guide 2024 for Beginners" is here to help you every step of the way. Embrace the OneDrive mindset and discover a new level of efficiency and organization in your digital life.

CONTENTS

CHAPTER 1: INTRODUCING TO ONEDRIVE

1.1 WHAT IS ONEDRIVE?

In today's digital age, efficient and secure file storage and sharing solutions are essential. Microsoft OneDrive is a cloud storage service that allows users to store, sync, and share files with ease. It integrates seamlessly with Microsoft Office and provides users with access to their files from any device, anywhere, at any time.

OneDrive began as Windows Live Folders in August 2007, later becoming known as SkyDrive before rebranding to OneDrive in 2014. This evolution reflects Microsoft's commitment to creating a robust and user-friendly cloud storage solution. OneDrive serves as a central hub for storing personal and professional files, offering features that cater to individual users, businesses, and enterprises.

One of the standout features of OneDrive is its seamless integration with Microsoft Office applications such as Word, Excel, and PowerPoint. This integration allows users to open, edit, and save documents directly to OneDrive from within these applications. Changes made to a document are automatically saved and synchronized across all devices linked to the OneDrive account, ensuring that users always have the latest version of their files at their fingertips.

OneDrive provides several layers of accessibility. Users can access their files through the OneDrive website, the desktop application for Windows and Mac, and mobile apps for iOS and Android devices. This cross-platform compatibility ensures that whether you're working from a laptop, tablet, or smartphone, your files are always within reach.

Security is a top priority for OneDrive. Microsoft employs advanced encryption methods to protect data both at rest and in transit. Files stored on OneDrive are encrypted using BitLocker, and data transfers are protected using SSL. Additionally, OneDrive offers Personal Vault, a protected area within OneDrive that adds an extra layer of security for your most sensitive files. Personal Vault uses two-step identity verification, ensuring that only you can access these files.

OneDrive also excels in file sharing and collaboration. Users can easily share files and folders with others by generating shareable links or by directly inviting individuals via email. Permissions can be set to control whether recipients can view or edit the files. This feature is particularly useful for team projects, allowing multiple people to collaborate on the same document simultaneously. Any changes made by collaborators are instantly synchronized, and version history is maintained so users can revert to previous versions if needed.

Storage capacity is another key aspect of OneDrive. While free accounts come with 5 GB of storage, various subscription plans offer increased storage capacity. For instance, Microsoft 365 Personal includes 1 TB of OneDrive storage, along with access to Office applications and other premium features. Business and enterprise plans offer even more storage, tailored to meet the needs of organizations of all sizes.

OneDrive's integration with Microsoft 365 extends beyond just storage. It works in harmony with other Microsoft services like Teams, SharePoint, and Outlook. This ecosystem approach allows for a cohesive and streamlined workflow, enhancing productivity and collaboration across different platforms and applications.

Another noteworthy feature of OneDrive is its offline access capability. Users can select specific files or folders to be available offline. This means that even without an internet connection, users can access and work on their files. Once the device reconnects to the internet, OneDrive automatically syncs the changes made offline.

OneDrive also supports automatic photo and video backup from mobile devices. This feature is particularly beneficial for users who want to ensure that their memories are safely stored in the cloud. Photos and videos can be organized into albums, and OneDrive's AI-powered search makes it easy to find specific images based on content, location, or tags.

In addition to personal use, OneDrive offers robust solutions for businesses. OneDrive for Business provides enterprise-level security, compliance, and administration features. IT administrators can manage user access, enforce data protection policies, and monitor usage through a centralized admin console. This ensures that organizational data remains secure while enabling employees to collaborate effectively.

In summary, Microsoft OneDrive is a versatile and secure cloud storage service designed to meet the needs of individual users and businesses alike. Its integration with Microsoft Office, cross-platform accessibility, robust security features, and collaborative capabilities make it an essential tool in the modern digital landscape. Whether you need to store personal files, collaborate on team projects, or manage enterprise data, OneDrive offers a comprehensive solution that simplifies and enhances your digital experience.

1.2 DEVELOPMENT HISTORY OF ONEDRIVE

The development history of OneDrive is a fascinating journey that showcases Microsoft's commitment to innovation and adaptation in the rapidly evolving field of cloud storage. From its inception as a simple file storage service to its current status as a comprehensive cloud solution integrated with Microsoft 365, OneDrive's evolution reflects the broader technological trends and user needs over the past two decades.

Early Beginnings: Windows Live Folders (2007)

OneDrive's story begins in August 2007 when it was first introduced as Windows Live Folders, part of the Windows Live suite of applications. At its launch, Windows Live Folders offered users 500 MB of free storage, a modest amount by today's standards but quite significant at the time. The service allowed users to store, share, and access files over the internet, marking Microsoft's initial foray into cloud storage.

Rebranding to SkyDrive (2008-2014)

In 2008, Windows Live Folders was rebranded to SkyDrive, a name that would become well-known among early adopters of cloud storage technology. The rebranding came with a substantial increase in free storage capacity to 5 GB, along with improved file-sharing capabilities. SkyDrive's web interface was designed to be user-friendly, with drag-and-drop functionality that made it easier to manage files and folders.

During this period, SkyDrive underwent several updates that expanded its functionality and integration with other Microsoft products. Notably, the service was integrated with Microsoft Office Web Apps in 2010, allowing users to create, edit, and share Office documents directly from their web browsers. This integration was a significant step in enhancing SkyDrive's appeal to both individual users and businesses.

Legal Challenges and the Birth of OneDrive (2014)

SkyDrive's journey was not without challenges. In 2013, a legal dispute with British broadcaster BSkyB over the "Sky" trademark forced Microsoft to rebrand its cloud storage service once again. In February 2014, SkyDrive officially became OneDrive. This rebranding was accompanied by several enhancements, including increased free storage (up to 15 GB for new users) and new features such as automatic photo and video backup from mobile devices.

The transition to OneDrive also marked a renewed focus on mobile accessibility and cross-platform compatibility. Microsoft released dedicated OneDrive apps for iOS and Android, in addition to its existing Windows and Windows Phone apps. This move ensured that users could access their files from virtually any device, fostering greater flexibility and convenience.

Integration with Microsoft 365 (2014-Present)

One of the most significant milestones in OneDrive's development history was its integration with Microsoft 365 (formerly Office 365). This integration transformed OneDrive from a standalone cloud storage service into a central component of Microsoft's productivity suite. Subscribers to Microsoft 365 gained access to 1 TB of OneDrive storage, along with premium features such as advanced file sharing, offline access, and ransomware detection and recovery.

This integration also facilitated seamless collaboration and productivity. Users could create, edit, and share Office documents directly from OneDrive, with real-time co-authoring capabilities that enabled multiple users to work on the same document simultaneously. This collaborative feature proved invaluable for remote teams and organizations, especially during the global shift towards remote work in the wake of the COVID-19 pandemic.

Enhanced Security and Compliance Features

As data security and privacy concerns became increasingly prominent, Microsoft invested heavily in enhancing OneDrive's security and compliance features. OneDrive introduced Personal Vault in 2019, a protected area within OneDrive that required two-step verification to access. This feature provided an extra layer of security for sensitive files such as identification documents and financial records.

For business and enterprise users, OneDrive for Business offered advanced security and compliance tools, including data loss prevention, eDiscovery, and advanced threat protection. IT administrators could enforce policies, monitor usage, and ensure regulatory compliance through a centralized admin console, making OneDrive a trusted solution for organizations with stringent security requirements.

Continued Innovation and Future Directions

Microsoft has continually updated and improved OneDrive to keep pace with evolving user needs and technological advancements. Recent updates have introduced features such as differential sync, which reduces bandwidth usage by only syncing changes to files, and enhanced photo management tools that leverage AI to organize and search images more effectively.

Looking ahead, Microsoft is likely to focus on further integrating OneDrive with its growing ecosystem of cloud services and artificial intelligence technologies. Future updates may include even more sophisticated collaboration tools, deeper integration with Microsoft Teams, and enhanced capabilities for managing and analyzing large volumes of data.

Conclusion

The development history of OneDrive is a testament to Microsoft's ability to adapt and innovate in response to changing technological landscapes and user demands. From its early days as Windows Live Folders to its current role as a cornerstone of Microsoft 365, OneDrive has continually evolved to provide users with a reliable, secure, and versatile cloud storage solution. As cloud technology continues to advance, OneDrive is well-positioned to remain at the forefront of digital storage and collaboration.

1.3 SUBSCRIPTION PLANS AND PRICING

Understanding the subscription plans and pricing of Microsoft OneDrive is essential for anyone looking to leverage its powerful cloud storage and collaboration capabilities. Whether you're an individual seeking reliable storage for personal files, a student needing tools for academic work, or a business professional aiming to enhance productivity, OneDrive offers a range of plans tailored to different needs and budgets. This section explores the various subscription options, their features, and pricing structures, helping you make an informed decision about which plan suits you best.

OneDrive Free Plan

For users who require basic cloud storage without any associated costs, Microsoft offers a free OneDrive plan. This plan provides 5 GB of storage space, which is suitable for storing essential documents, photos, and small files. The free plan is a great starting point for users new to cloud storage or those with minimal storage needs. It includes basic features such as file sharing, syncing across devices, and access to OneDrive's web interface and mobile apps. However, the free plan lacks some of the advanced features available in paid plans, making it less suitable for heavy users or those requiring extensive storage and collaboration tools.

OneDrive Standalone Plans

Microsoft offers standalone OneDrive plans for users who need more storage without the additional features of Microsoft 365. These plans provide increased storage capacity and enhanced functionality:

- **OneDrive 100 GB**: For $1.99 per month, this plan offers 100 GB of storage space. It is ideal for users with moderate storage needs, such as storing large photo libraries, videos, and important documents. The plan includes the ability to sync files across multiple devices, share files and folders with others, and access files offline.

Microsoft 365 Personal

For individuals seeking a comprehensive suite of productivity tools alongside expanded OneDrive storage, the Microsoft 365 Personal plan is an excellent choice. Priced at $69.99 per year or $6.99 per month, this plan includes 1 TB of OneDrive storage. Additionally, subscribers gain access to the full suite of Microsoft Office applications, including Word, Excel, PowerPoint, Outlook, and OneNote, both online and offline.

The Microsoft 365 Personal plan also includes premium features such as advanced file sharing options, ransomware detection and recovery, and offline access to files. Subscribers can install Office applications on up to five devices, including PCs, Macs, tablets, and smartphones. This plan is perfect for individuals who need a versatile and powerful set of tools for personal, academic, or professional use.

Microsoft 365 Family

Designed for households with multiple users, the Microsoft 365 Family plan offers a cost-effective solution for families or small groups. Priced at $99.99 per year or $9.99 per month, this plan includes 1 TB of OneDrive storage per user, for up to six users. Each user also gains access to the full suite of Microsoft Office applications and premium features.

The Family plan allows each member to install Office applications on multiple devices and includes additional benefits such as parental controls, advanced security features, and collaborative tools for shared projects. This plan is ideal for families, roommates, or small teams who need to share resources while maintaining individual storage and workspace.

OneDrive for Business

For businesses and enterprises, Microsoft offers OneDrive for Business plans that provide robust storage solutions, advanced security, and enterprise-grade collaboration tools. These plans are designed to meet the needs of organizations of all sizes, from small businesses to large corporations:

- **OneDrive for Business Plan 1**: Priced at $5 per user per month, this plan includes 1 TB of storage per user. It offers file sharing, synchronization, and access to Office Online applications (Word, Excel, PowerPoint, and OneNote). This plan is suitable for businesses that need basic cloud storage and collaboration tools without the full suite of Office applications.

- **OneDrive for Business Plan 2**: For $10 per user per month, this plan provides unlimited storage per user (for subscriptions with five or more users). It includes advanced security features such as data loss prevention, advanced threat protection, and compliance tools. Users also gain access to Office Online applications and enhanced file sharing and collaboration capabilities.

Microsoft 365 Business Plans

For businesses requiring a comprehensive productivity suite alongside OneDrive storage, Microsoft 365 Business plans offer a complete solution:

- **Microsoft 365 Business Basic**: At $6 per user per month, this plan includes 1 TB of OneDrive storage per user, access to Office Online applications, Microsoft Teams, Exchange, and SharePoint. It is ideal for businesses that need essential productivity tools and cloud services.

- **Microsoft 365 Business Standard**: Priced at $12.50 per user per month, this plan includes 1 TB of OneDrive storage per user and access to the full suite of Office applications for desktop and mobile. It also includes Microsoft Teams, Exchange, and SharePoint, making it suitable for businesses that require robust collaboration and productivity tools.

- **Microsoft 365 Business Premium**: At $22 per user per month, this plan offers 1 TB of OneDrive storage per user, access to the full suite of Office applications, and advanced security features such as Microsoft Defender, conditional access, and identity protection. This plan is ideal for businesses that require the highest level of security and comprehensive productivity tools.

Conclusion

Microsoft OneDrive's subscription plans and pricing are designed to cater to a wide range of users, from individuals with basic storage needs to businesses requiring advanced security and collaboration tools. By offering various plans with different features and storage capacities, OneDrive ensures that users can find a solution that fits their specific requirements and budget. Whether you're looking to store personal files, collaborate on projects, or manage enterprise data, OneDrive provides a flexible and reliable cloud storage solution.

1.4 HOW TO PURCHASE A ONEDRIVE SUBSCRIPTION

Purchasing a OneDrive subscription is a straightforward process that ensures you have access to Microsoft's comprehensive cloud storage and productivity tools. Whether you need additional storage for personal use, a suite of Office applications for your family, or enterprise-level solutions for your business, OneDrive offers a variety of subscription plans to meet your needs. This section provides a detailed guide on how to purchase a OneDrive subscription, from selecting the right plan to completing the purchase and setting up your account.

Step 1: Determine Your Needs

Before purchasing a OneDrive subscription, it's essential to evaluate your storage and productivity requirements. Consider the following factors:

- **Storage Needs**: Estimate the amount of storage you need. A free plan might suffice for minimal storage needs, but if you have extensive files, photos, or videos, a paid plan with more storage might be necessary.

- **Productivity Tools**: If you need access to Microsoft Office applications like Word, Excel, and PowerPoint, consider a Microsoft 365 plan that includes these tools.

- **Number of Users**: Determine if you need a plan for a single user or multiple users. Microsoft 365 Family plans provide storage and productivity tools for up to six users.

- **Business Requirements**: If you're purchasing for a business, consider features like advanced security, compliance tools, and collaboration capabilities offered in OneDrive for Business plans.

Step 2: Explore Subscription Plans

Microsoft offers various OneDrive and Microsoft 365 subscription plans. Here's a quick overview:

- **OneDrive Basic**: Free plan with 5 GB of storage.

- **OneDrive Standalone**: 100 GB for $1.99 per month.

- **Microsoft 365 Personal**: 1 TB of OneDrive storage and access to Office applications for $69.99 per year or $6.99 per month.

- **Microsoft 365 Family**: 1 TB per user for up to six users and access to Office applications for $99.99 per year or $9.99 per month.

- **OneDrive for Business Plan 1**: 1 TB per user for $5 per user per month.

- **OneDrive for Business Plan 2**: Unlimited storage per user for $10 per user per month.

- **Microsoft 365 Business Plans**: Various plans offering OneDrive storage, Office applications, and advanced security features.

Step 3: Visit the OneDrive Website

To purchase a subscription, start by visiting the OneDrive website. Here, you can explore different plans, compare features, and select the one that best suits your needs. The website provides detailed information about each plan, including pricing, storage capacity, and included features.

Step 4: Select Your Plan

Once you've determined the plan that meets your needs, click on the "Buy Now" or "Subscribe" button associated with that plan. This will take you to a page where you can review the plan details and proceed with your purchase.

Step 5: Sign In or Create a Microsoft Account

To purchase a OneDrive subscription, you need a Microsoft account. If you already have one, sign in with your credentials. If not, you'll need to create a new Microsoft account. This account will be used to manage your subscription and access OneDrive.

Step 6: Enter Payment Information

After signing in or creating your account, you'll be prompted to enter your payment information. Microsoft accepts various payment methods, including credit cards, debit cards, and PayPal. Enter your payment details and ensure that your billing information is accurate.

Step 7: Review and Confirm Your Purchase

Before finalizing your purchase, review the subscription details, including the plan you've selected, the storage capacity, the cost, and the billing frequency (monthly or annually). Once you've confirmed that everything is correct, click on the "Confirm" or "Purchase" button to complete your transaction.

Step 8: Set Up Your OneDrive Subscription

After purchasing your subscription, you'll receive a confirmation email with details about your plan and payment. Follow the instructions in the email to set up your OneDrive account. If you've purchased a plan that includes Microsoft Office applications, you'll also receive instructions on how to download and install these applications on your devices.

Step 9: Install OneDrive on Your Devices

To make the most of your OneDrive subscription, install the OneDrive app on all your devices. This includes your desktop computer, laptop, tablet, and smartphone. The OneDrive app is available for Windows, macOS, iOS, and Android. Installing the app allows you to sync files across your devices, access your files offline, and ensure that your documents are always up to date.

Step 10: Start Using OneDrive

With your subscription set up and the OneDrive app installed, you're ready to start using OneDrive. Upload files, organize your documents, share files and folders with others, and take advantage of the productivity tools included in your plan. If you've subscribed to a Microsoft 365 plan, explore the full suite of Office applications to enhance your productivity further.

Conclusion

Purchasing a OneDrive subscription is a straightforward process that offers tremendous benefits in terms of storage, accessibility, and productivity. By following these steps, you can easily select the right plan, complete your purchase, and set up your account to start enjoying the full range of features that OneDrive has to offer. Whether you're an individual user, part of a family, or managing a business, OneDrive provides a flexible and reliable solution to meet your cloud storage needs.

1.5 INSTALLATION METHODS FOR ONEDRIVE

Installing OneDrive on your devices is a crucial step to leverage its full potential, ensuring seamless access to your files from anywhere. Microsoft has made the installation process user-friendly across various platforms, including Windows, macOS, iOS, and Android. This section provides a comprehensive guide on how to install OneDrive on different devices, helping you get started with Microsoft's cloud storage service.

Installing OneDrive on Windows

OneDrive comes pre-installed on Windows 10 and Windows 11, making the setup process straightforward. If you're using an older version of Windows or need to reinstall OneDrive, follow these steps:

1. **Download OneDrive**: Visit the OneDrive download page and click on the "Download" button to get the latest version of OneDrive.

2. **Run the Installer**: Once the download is complete, open the installer file and

follow the on-screen instructions to install OneDrive.

3. **Sign In**: After installation, open OneDrive from the Start menu or taskbar. Sign in with your Microsoft account. If you don't have one, you'll need to create a new account.

4. **Set Up OneDrive**: Follow the setup prompts to choose the folders you want to sync with OneDrive. You can select specific folders or sync your entire PC.

5. **Sync Files**: OneDrive will start syncing your selected files. You can access these files through the OneDrive folder in File Explorer.

Installing OneDrive on macOS

For macOS users, installing OneDrive is a simple process:

1. **Download OneDrive**: Go to the OneDrive download page and click "Download."

2. **Install OneDrive**: Open the downloaded .pkg file and follow the installation instructions.

3. **Sign In**: After installation, launch OneDrive from the Applications folder. Sign in with your Microsoft account.

4. **Set Up OneDrive**: Follow the setup instructions to choose which folders to sync. You can also set the location of your OneDrive folder on your Mac.

5. **Sync Files**: OneDrive will begin syncing your chosen files. You can access them through the OneDrive folder in Finder.

Installing OneDrive on iOS

To use OneDrive on your iPhone or iPad, follow these steps:

1. **Download OneDrive**: Open the App Store on your device and search for "OneDrive." Tap "Get" to download and install the app.

2. **Sign In**: Launch the OneDrive app and sign in with your Microsoft account.

3. **Grant Permissions**: The app will request access to your photos, files, and notifications. Grant the necessary permissions to enable full functionality.

4. **Sync Files**: Once signed in, you can start uploading and syncing files. The app allows you to create new folders, upload files, and access files offline.

Installing OneDrive on Android

Android users can easily install OneDrive by following these steps:

1. **Download OneDrive**: Open the Google Play Store and search for "OneDrive." Tap "Install" to download the app.

2. **Sign In**: After installation, open the OneDrive app and sign in with your Microsoft account.

3. **Grant Permissions**: The app will request permissions to access your photos, media, and files. Grant these permissions to ensure full functionality.

4. **Sync Files**: You can now upload, sync, and access files on your Android device. The app also allows you to create new folders and share files with others.

Installing OneDrive for Business

For business users, OneDrive for Business provides additional features and security. Here's how to install it:

1. **Access Your Microsoft 365 Account**: Sign in to your Microsoft 365 account and navigate to the OneDrive section.

2. **Download OneDrive for Business**: Click on "Get the OneDrive apps" and download the OneDrive for Business installer.

3. **Install OneDrive for Business**: Open the downloaded installer file and follow the installation instructions.

4. **Sign In**: After installation, sign in with your work or school account associated with Microsoft 365.

5. **Set Up OneDrive**: Follow the setup instructions to select the folders you want to sync. You can choose specific folders or sync your entire business account.

6. **Sync Files**: OneDrive for Business will start syncing your selected files. Access these files through the OneDrive for Business folder on your computer.

Additional Tips for Installing OneDrive

- **Regular Updates**: Ensure that OneDrive is regularly updated to benefit from the latest features and security enhancements. Most devices will update OneDrive automatically, but you can check for updates manually if needed.

- **Troubleshooting**: If you encounter any issues during installation, Microsoft provides extensive support resources, including online guides and community forums. Additionally, the OneDrive app includes a built-in troubleshooter to help resolve common problems.

Conclusion

Installing OneDrive across different platforms is a simple and efficient process, enabling you to access your files anytime, anywhere. By following the steps outlined above, you can ensure a smooth installation experience on Windows, macOS, iOS, and Android devices. With OneDrive set up, you'll be ready to take full advantage of Microsoft's powerful cloud storage and collaboration tools, enhancing your productivity and keeping your files secure.

1.6 THE DESIGN CONCEPT BEHIND ONEDRIVE

The design concept behind OneDrive is grounded in simplicity, accessibility, and seamless integration, reflecting Microsoft's overarching philosophy of empowering users to achieve more. As a cloud storage service, OneDrive aims to offer a unified platform where individuals and businesses can store, sync, and share files efficiently. This section delves into the core principles that underpin the design of OneDrive, examining its user-centric approach, cross-platform functionality, integration with the Microsoft ecosystem, and the emphasis on security and collaboration.

User-Centric Approach

At the heart of OneDrive's design is a commitment to user-friendliness. Microsoft has prioritized creating an intuitive interface that makes it easy for users to navigate and manage their files. This is evident in the consistent design language across the web interface, desktop application, and mobile apps. The clean and straightforward layout ensures that users, regardless of their technical expertise, can quickly learn how to use OneDrive.

The interface features a familiar file and folder structure, akin to traditional file systems used on computers. This design choice reduces the learning curve, as users can organize their files in a way that mirrors their desktop environment. Additionally, OneDrive provides drag-and-drop functionality, making it simple to upload files and move them between folders.

Cross-Platform Functionality

OneDrive's design is inherently cross-platform, enabling users to access their files from any device with an internet connection. This flexibility is crucial in today's world, where individuals frequently switch between devices such as laptops, tablets, and smartphones. Microsoft has developed dedicated OneDrive apps for Windows, macOS, iOS, and Android, ensuring a consistent user experience across all platforms.

This cross-platform capability extends to the seamless synchronization of files. Any changes made to a file on one device are automatically synced across all devices linked to the user's OneDrive account. This real-time synchronization ensures that users always have access to the most up-to-date versions of their files, no matter where they are.

Integration with the Microsoft Ecosystem

OneDrive is designed to integrate seamlessly with the broader Microsoft ecosystem, enhancing its functionality and utility. This integration is a cornerstone of OneDrive's design, as it leverages the strengths of other Microsoft products to provide a cohesive user experience.

One of the most significant integrations is with Microsoft Office. Users can open, edit, and save Word, Excel, PowerPoint, and OneNote documents directly within OneDrive. This integration supports real-time collaboration, allowing multiple users to work on the same document simultaneously. Changes are tracked and synced instantly, and version history ensures that previous versions of documents can be restored if needed.

Furthermore, OneDrive is deeply integrated with Microsoft Teams, SharePoint, and Outlook. These integrations facilitate seamless file sharing and collaboration within organizations. For instance, files shared in Teams are stored in OneDrive, making it easy to manage and access them from one central location. Similarly, attachments in Outlook can be saved directly to OneDrive, streamlining email management and storage.

Emphasis on Security

Security is a paramount concern in the design of OneDrive. Microsoft employs robust security measures to protect user data, both at rest and in transit. OneDrive uses BitLocker encryption for data stored on Microsoft servers and SSL encryption for data being transferred between devices and the cloud.

OneDrive's security features include Personal Vault, a protected area within OneDrive that provides an extra layer of security for sensitive files. Personal Vault requires two-step verification to access and locks automatically after a period of inactivity. This feature is designed to safeguard critical documents such as identification papers, financial records, and personal photos.

For business users, OneDrive for Business offers enterprise-grade security and compliance features. These include data loss prevention, advanced threat protection, and eDiscovery capabilities. IT administrators can manage user access, enforce data protection policies, and monitor usage through a centralized admin console, ensuring that organizational data remains secure.

Focus on Collaboration

Collaboration is a key element of OneDrive's design, reflecting the growing need for team-oriented workflows in both personal and professional settings. OneDrive's sharing capabilities are designed to be straightforward and flexible, allowing users to share files and folders with others easily. Sharing options include generating shareable links or inviting specific individuals via email, with the ability to set permissions for viewing or editing.

OneDrive's collaborative features are further enhanced by its integration with Microsoft Office. Users can co-author documents in real-time, with changes synced instantly. Comments and track changes are supported, enabling clear communication and feedback within the document. These features make OneDrive an invaluable tool for group projects, remote work, and any scenario where multiple individuals need to collaborate on the same files.

Conclusion

The design concept behind OneDrive is rooted in the principles of simplicity, accessibility, and integration. By prioritizing user experience, cross-platform functionality, seamless integration with the Microsoft ecosystem, robust security measures, and collaborative capabilities, OneDrive offers a comprehensive and user-friendly cloud storage solution. These design principles ensure that OneDrive meets the diverse needs of individuals and businesses, empowering them to store, sync, and share files with ease and confidence.

1.7 ADOPTING THE ONEDRIVE MINDSET

Adopting the OneDrive mindset involves embracing a new way of managing, accessing, and sharing files that leverages the full potential of cloud technology. This shift not only enhances productivity but also ensures data security and accessibility across various devices. To fully benefit from OneDrive, users must understand its core principles and integrate them into their daily workflows. This section explores the essential aspects of adopting the OneDrive mindset, focusing on convenience, collaboration, security, and integration.

Convenience and Accessibility

OneDrive is designed to offer unparalleled convenience and accessibility. By storing files in the cloud, users can access their documents, photos, and videos from any device with an internet connection. This eliminates the need for physical storage devices such as USB drives and external hard drives, reducing the risk of data loss due to hardware failure or misplacement.

Adopting the OneDrive mindset means getting accustomed to accessing files via the OneDrive app or web interface rather than relying solely on local storage. This approach ensures that your files are always available, whether you're working from your office, home, or on the go. The OneDrive mobile apps for iOS and Android further enhance this convenience by providing instant access to your files wherever you are.

Seamless Synchronization

One of the key benefits of OneDrive is its ability to synchronize files across multiple devices in real-time. This feature ensures that any changes made to a file on one device are automatically reflected on all other devices linked to the same OneDrive account. Adopting this aspect of OneDrive requires users to trust the synchronization process and recognize that their files are consistently up-to-date across all platforms.

To make the most of this feature, users should regularly save their work to OneDrive rather than local storage. This practice not only ensures that files are backed up in the cloud but also allows for seamless transitions between devices. For instance, you can start a document on your desktop computer at work, continue editing it on your tablet during your commute, and finish it on your laptop at home without any manual file transfers.

Enhanced Collaboration

Embracing the OneDrive mindset also involves leveraging its robust collaboration tools. OneDrive allows users to share files and folders with others, enabling real-time collaboration on documents, spreadsheets, and presentations. This is particularly valuable for team projects, remote work, and any scenario where multiple individuals need to contribute to the same files.

To effectively adopt this collaborative approach, users should familiarize themselves with OneDrive's sharing options. You can generate shareable links or invite specific individuals via email, setting permissions for viewing or editing as needed. Real-time co-authoring features in Microsoft Office applications further enhance collaboration by allowing multiple users to work on the same document simultaneously, with changes synchronized instantly.

Security and Data Protection

Security is a fundamental aspect of the OneDrive mindset. Microsoft employs advanced encryption methods to protect data both at rest and in transit, ensuring that your files remain secure. Additionally, features like Personal Vault provide an extra layer of protection for sensitive files, requiring two-step verification to access.

Adopting the OneDrive mindset involves understanding and utilizing these security features to safeguard your data. Regularly updating passwords, enabling two-factor authentication, and being mindful of sharing permissions are all practices that contribute to a secure cloud environment. For business users, OneDrive for Business offers additional security measures such as data loss prevention and compliance tools, which IT administrators can manage to protect organizational data.

Integration with Microsoft Ecosystem

OneDrive's seamless integration with the broader Microsoft ecosystem is another key aspect of its design. This integration enhances productivity by allowing users to work within a unified platform that includes Microsoft Office, Teams, SharePoint, and more. Adopting the OneDrive mindset means taking full advantage of these integrations to streamline workflows and improve efficiency.

For example, files stored in OneDrive can be easily accessed and shared within Microsoft Teams, facilitating communication and collaboration among team members. Similarly, OneDrive's integration with Outlook allows for easy attachment management, enabling users to save email attachments directly to OneDrive for organized storage and quick access.

Adopting Best Practices

To fully embrace the OneDrive mindset, users should adopt best practices that maximize the platform's benefits:

1. **Organize Your Files**: Maintain a structured folder system within OneDrive to keep your files organized and easily accessible.

2. **Regular Backups**: Ensure that important files are regularly backed up to OneDrive to protect against data loss.

3. **Utilize Offline Access**: Enable offline access for critical files, allowing you to work on them even without an internet connection.

4. **Stay Updated**: Keep the OneDrive app and related software up-to-date to benefit from the latest features and security enhancements.

Conclusion

Adopting the OneDrive mindset involves more than just using a cloud storage service; it requires a shift in how you manage, access, and share your files. By embracing the convenience, synchronization, collaboration, security, and integration that OneDrive offers, users can significantly enhance their productivity and ensure their data is always accessible and secure. Integrating these principles into your daily workflow will help you make the most of Microsoft OneDrive and its powerful capabilities.

1.8 FUTURE USES AND POTENTIAL OF ONEDRIVE

The future of Microsoft OneDrive is promising, with significant potential for growth and innovation. As cloud storage and collaboration technologies continue to evolve, OneDrive is poised to become an even more integral part of both personal and professional digital lives. This section explores the future uses and potential of OneDrive, highlighting emerging trends, anticipated advancements, and how OneDrive might continue to adapt to the changing landscape of technology.

Enhanced Integration with AI and Machine Learning

One of the most exciting prospects for the future of OneDrive is its integration with artificial intelligence (AI) and machine learning (ML). Microsoft has already begun incorporating AI into its cloud services, and this trend is expected to grow. AI can enhance OneDrive in several ways:

- **Improved Search Capabilities**: AI-powered search will make it easier for users to find files quickly, even within large and complex directories. By understanding context and using natural language processing, OneDrive will be able to deliver more accurate search results.

- **Automated Organization**: Machine learning algorithms can help users organize their files more efficiently. For instance, OneDrive could automatically categorize documents, photos, and videos based on content and usage patterns, reducing the need for manual organization.

- **Smart Recommendations**: AI could provide intelligent recommendations for file management, such as suggesting files that might need attention, highlighting documents that are frequently accessed, or identifying duplicates to free up space.

Deeper Integration with Microsoft 365 and Beyond

As part of the Microsoft 365 suite, OneDrive's integration with other Microsoft services is likely to deepen. This integration will further streamline workflows and enhance productivity:

- **Teams Integration**: OneDrive will continue to enhance its integration with Microsoft Teams, enabling seamless file sharing, collaboration, and storage within the Teams environment. This will support remote and hybrid work models by providing a unified platform for communication and document management.

- **SharePoint Enhancements**: Integration with SharePoint will likely see improvements, making it easier for organizations to manage content and collaborate on projects. Enhanced synchronization and sharing capabilities will benefit large enterprises with complex data management needs.

- **Outlook Synergy**: OneDrive's integration with Outlook could be enhanced to allow for more intuitive attachment handling, automated categorization of email attachments, and streamlined access to shared files directly from the email interface.

Expansion of Security Features

Security is a paramount concern in the digital age, and OneDrive is expected to continue evolving to meet these challenges. Future enhancements may include:

- **Advanced Encryption**: Microsoft will likely adopt even more advanced encryption methods to protect user data both at rest and in transit. This could include quantum-resistant encryption algorithms as quantum computing becomes more prevalent.

- **Zero Trust Architecture**: Implementing a Zero Trust security model, where trust is never assumed and always verified, could become a standard for OneDrive. This would involve continuous authentication and authorization of users and devices accessing OneDrive.

- **Enhanced Compliance Tools**: For businesses, OneDrive will continue to develop tools to ensure compliance with evolving data protection regulations such as GDPR, CCPA, and others. This will be crucial for organizations operating in highly regulated industries.

Innovative Collaboration Features

As remote work and global collaboration become more common, OneDrive is expected to introduce innovative features that facilitate teamwork and communication:

- **Real-Time Editing Enhancements**: OneDrive will likely improve real-time collaboration features, making it easier for multiple users to edit documents simultaneously without conflicts. Enhanced version control and change tracking will support smoother collaborative workflows.

- **Virtual Collaboration Spaces**: Integration with virtual and augmented reality platforms could allow teams to collaborate in immersive virtual environments. This could be particularly useful for design, engineering, and creative industries.

- **Enhanced Mobile Collaboration**: As mobile work becomes increasingly prevalent, OneDrive's mobile apps will continue to evolve, offering robust collaboration tools that are optimized for smartphones and tablets.

Green Technology and Sustainability

Sustainability and environmental impact are becoming critical considerations in technology development. OneDrive is expected to align with Microsoft's broader sustainability goals:

- **Energy-Efficient Data Centers**: Microsoft is investing in energy-efficient data centers powered by renewable energy sources. OneDrive's infrastructure will benefit from these advancements, reducing its carbon footprint.

- **Eco-Friendly Features**: Future updates to OneDrive may include features that promote sustainable practices, such as tools for tracking and reducing digital waste or recommendations for eco-friendly file management.

Personalization and User Experience

User experience and personalization will remain key focus areas for OneDrive:

- **Customizable Interfaces**: Users will likely have more options to customize the OneDrive interface to suit their preferences, improving usability and satisfaction.

- **Personalized Insights**: Leveraging AI, OneDrive could provide personalized insights and analytics, helping users understand their storage patterns, usage trends, and opportunities for optimization.

Conclusion

The future uses and potential of OneDrive are vast and exciting. With advancements in AI, deeper integration with Microsoft 365, enhanced security features, innovative collaboration tools, and a focus on sustainability, OneDrive is set to remain a leading cloud storage and collaboration solution. By adopting these new technologies and trends, OneDrive will continue to evolve, providing users with powerful, secure, and efficient tools to manage and collaborate on their digital content. Whether for personal use or within a business context, OneDrive's future developments promise to enhance productivity, streamline workflows, and ensure that users' data is always accessible and protected.

CHAPTER 2: KEYBOARD SHORTCUTS IN ONEDRIVE

WINDOWS

Frequently used shortcuts

To do this	Press
Rename the selected item.	F2
Delete the selected item(s).	Delete
Close the current pop-up or item.	Esc
Download a selected item.	Ctrl+S
Share the selected file or folder.	S
Open the context menu for the selected item.	Shift+F10 or the Windows Menu key

Navigate in OneDrive for work or school

To do this	Press
Move between OneDrive regions.	Tab key or Shift+Tab
Move through the tree view navigation pane.	Up or Down arrow key
Move through the contents grid file pane.	Up or Down arrow key

Select or clear items

To do this	Press
Select an adjacent item.	Arrow keys
Select all items when the focus is in the contents grid.	Ctrl+A
Deselect the item(s) when the focus is in the contents grid.	Ctrl+D
Clear all or navigate to the previous folder.	Esc
Select a file or folder in the contents grid or clear the selection.	Spacebar

Display information

To do this	Press
Refresh the window.	F5
Switch between the **List** and **Thumbnails** view of the contents grid.	V
In the **List** view of the contents grid, get details about a selected file.	Up or Down arrow key
Display keyboard shortcuts.	?
Toggle details pane.	I

Manage files and folders

To do this	Press
Open or download the item.	Enter
Download the selected item.	Ctrl+S
Rename the selected file or folder.	F2
Share the selected file or folder.	S
Delete the selected file(s) or folder(s).	Delete

WEB

Frequently used shortcuts

To do this	Press
Display keyboard shortcuts.	?
Select all items when the focus is in the content grid.	Ctrl+A
Deselect the item(s) when the focus is in the content grid.	Ctrl+D
Clear all or navigate to the previous folder.	Esc
Select the adjacent item.	Arrow keys
Toggle selection for the current item.	Spacebar
Open the selected item.	Enter
Open a document from an internet site.	Ctrl+O, type, paste, or select a URL, and then Enter.

To do this	Press
Download the selected item.	Shift+F10 or Windows Menu key, then Down arrow key or Tab key until you reach the **Download** option, and then Enter.
Delete the selected item.	Delete
Share the selected folder or file.	S
Rename the selected file.	F2
Refresh the window.	F5
Toggle details pane.	I

Navigate in OneDrive for work or school

To do this	Press
Move between the browser bar and OneDrive.	F6 or Ctrl+F6
Move between the OneDrive regions.	Tab key or Shift+Tab
Move through the list of items (in the **Navigation** pane or **Files** list).	Up or Down arrow key
Get information about the selected file, for example, the file name (in the **Files** list).	Right or Left arrow key
Open the context menu for the selected item.	Shift+F10 or Windows Menu key

CHAPTER 3: SETTING UP ONEDRIVE

Microsoft OneDrive stands as a beacon of cloud storage, embodying convenience, and security for users worldwide. This chapter dives into the essentials of OneDrive, guiding you through the initial steps to harness its full potential. OneDrive is not just another storage option; it's a gateway to accessing your files anytime, anywhere.

OneDrive makes life easier. You can start by setting up your account. This step is your entry into a world where your documents, photos, and files move with you. It's about breaking free from the physical constraints of hard drives and USB sticks.

Understanding the OneDrive interface is like learning the controls of a new car. Once you know where everything is, the drive becomes smooth and effortless. This chapter will show you the dashboard, the buttons, and how to navigate through your digital files as if you were browsing through your own memories.

OneDrive basics covers more than just saving files. It's about creating a digital environment that's organized, accessible, and secure. Here, you'll learn how to upload your first file, create folders, and set up your space. It's like setting up your room where everything has its place, making it easier to find when you need it.

SETTING UP YOUR ACCOUNT

Getting started with Microsoft OneDrive is like opening a door to a room where all your files live safely and can be reached from anywhere. OneDrive is a place on the internet, made by Microsoft, where you can keep your pictures, documents, and more. Think of it as your digital drawer that you can open from any computer, phone, or tablet as long as you're connected to the internet.

1. **Find OneDrive Online:** Goto the Microsoft One Drive website using any internet browser. This is where you'll start setting up your new space for storing files.

2. **Choose to Sign Up:** You need a Microsoft account to use OneDrive. If you have an email with Outlook.com or have used Micro- soft services before, you're all set. If not, creating a new account is easy and free. Look for a button or link that says "Sign Up," "Create One" or "Create Account." Click on it to begin the process of making your OneDrive account.

3. **Enter Your Information:** Microsoft will ask for some details. You'll need to give your name and choose an email address to use with your account. If you already have an email you want to use, you can enter that. Then, pick a password. Th is password is like a secret code that only you should know.

By signing up with your Microsoft account, you can use OneDrive on your desktops or mobile devices. The OneDrive app is pre-installed on Windows and Mac computers. You can also download it from the Apple App Store or Micros oft 's website. OneDrive's in-terface is easy to navigate and has fields for documents, e-mails, and music.

1. **Prove You're Not a Robot:** Sometimes, Microsoft wants to make sure a real person is signing up. They might ask you to type in some letters or numbers you see on the screen, or select certain pictures. This step helps keep robots out of OneDrive.
2. **Verify Your Email or Phone:** After giving your details, Microsoft sends a code to your email or phone. This code is a way to check that you gave them the right information. Find the code and enter it on the website where Microsoft tells you to.
3. **Explore OneDrive:** Once your account is set up, you might see a welcome message or a tour. This is a good way to learn where things are in OneDrive, like how to upload files or make new folders.
4. **Choose Automatic File Saving (Optional**): OneDrive can automatically save copies of your files. This means if something hap- pens to your computer, your files are still safe in OneDrive. Decide if you want this option and select it if you do.
5. **Upload Your First File:** To start using OneDrive, try uploading a file. You can drag files into the OneDrive folder on your com-puter or use the website to select files from your computer to upload.
6. **Create Folders**: Organize your files by creating folders. You might want a folder for school projects, one for photos, and another for important documents. Creating folders helps you keep your files neat and easy to find.
7. **Share Files or Folders**: If you want to share something with friends, family, or classmates, OneDrive makes it easy. Select the file or folder you want to share, then choose how you want to share it. You can send a link by email or get a link to share how- ever you like.
8. **Use OneDrive with Microsoft Apps**: One Drive works with Microsoft Word, PowerPoint, and other apps. You can start a docu-ment right in OneDrive, and it's saved automatically. This is great for working on projects from anywhere.
9. **Access Your Files Anywhere:** Even if you're not on your own computer, you can get to your OneDrive files. Just go to the OneDrive website and sign in. All your files will be there, waiting for you.
10. **Check Your Privacy Settings:** OneDrive lets you control who sees your files. Take a look at the privacy settings to ensure your files are shared only how you want them to be.
11. **Upgrade Your Storage If Needed: Start** with some free storage space. If you find you need more, OneDrive offers options to get more space for a fee. It's like expanding your digital room to fit more things.
12. **Keep Your Files Safe**: Remember, OneDrive is your space on the internet for keeping files safe and accessible from anywhere. Enjoy the peace of mind knowing your files are secure and always with you.

NAVIGATING THE ONEDRIVE INTERFACE

To download OneDrive, you can download the app from an app store or go directly to the Microsoft website. You'll also need your Microsoft account details, as well as your Microsoft password. You can create an account for free or pay a monthly fee. The interface will automatically save your documents; you can access them anytime.

Another feature that you can use to save space is Files on Demand. When you don't have access to the internet, you can use OneDrive to edit your files offline. OneDrive will automatically store changes. It's helpful if you're on a limited amount of storage. This feature also means that you can access your files on any device that can access your Microsoft account.

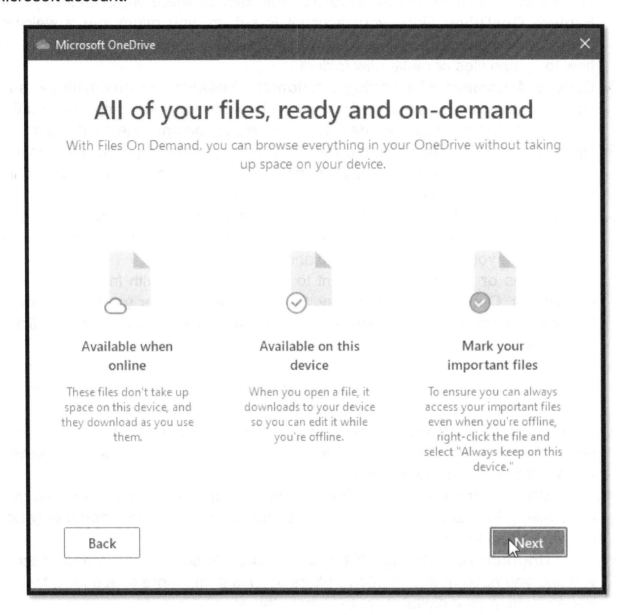

MS OneDrive is pre-installed on Windows computers, making it more convenient. It's also easier to set up than other cloud storage services. Once you've installed it, you'll see a folder on your computer called "OneDrive." After logging in with your Microsoft account, you can upload files to OneDrive.

Here is the general layout of the MS OneDrive interface.

- **Navigation Bar or Pane:** Anchoring the left side of OneDrive's interface, the navigation bar serves as your compass through the cloud. It neatly categorizes your digital repository into sections like Files, Shared, Recent, and Photos, among others, making navigation intuitive.

- **Main Window (Central Viewing Area):** The heart of OneDrive's interface, this central space, presents the contents of which-ever folder or section you've selected from the navigation bar. Depending on your preference, you can view the files & folders arranged in a tidy grid or a detailed list.

- **Utility Toolbar:** Perched atop the interface, the toolbar is your toolkit for file management. It's where you'll find essential func-tions such as Upload, Share, Sync, and New. This toolbar might also house a search feature, streamlining the process of locating your files or folders in the large digital ocean.

- **File/Folder (Contextual) Options:** Clicking on a file or folder reveals a suite of actions specific to your selection. These actions, accessible via a right-click or a contextual toolbar, empower you to rename, move, delete, share, download, or explore into the properties of your files and folders.

- **More Actions Menu:** Symbolized by three dots(ellipsis), this menu extends your command over your files and folders, offering additional management options like copy, move, rename, delete, and share. It's a quick-access point for more nuanced file handling.

- **File Preview Pane**: Certain views within OneDrive might include a preview pane, allowing you to peek into the contents of a file without fully opening it. This feature is particularly useful for swiftly checking the contents of documents, photos, or other files.

- **Notifications and Customization / Settings:** OneDrive keeps you informed with notifications about sync status, updates on shared files, and other pertinent information. The settings and account options, typically symbolized by a gear or profile icon, let you tailor OneDrive to your liking, ensuring a personalized cloud experience.

ONEDRIVE BASICS

OneDrive serves as a digital safe space, where every file and document you hold dear is stored securely in the cloud. Imagine having a magic box where everything important can be kept, and this magic box is OneDrive. It's a place where your digital life can be orga-nized, accessed, and shared easily, regardless of where you are or what device you're using. Here's how to tap into the fundamental powers of OneDrive:

1. **Uploading Files:** Think of OneDrive as your cloud-based flash drive. Uploading files to OneDrive is as simple as dragging them from your computer into the OneDrive folder or using the upload button on the website. It's like moving your physical files into a virtual drawer you can open from anywhere.

2. **Creating Folders:** Organizing your files in OneDrive is made easy with folders. Just like you would organize documents into folders in a filing cabinet, you can create folders in OneDrive to keep your digital files neat and tidy. This way, finding what you need when you need it, becomes a breeze.

3. **Setting Up Your Space:** Personalizing your OneDrive space is like setting up your own digital room. You can decide how your files are arranged, which files or folders should be shared, and which ones remain private. It's about making OneDrive work for you, tailored to your needs and preferences.

4. **Sharing Files and Folders:** OneDrive shines when it comes to sharing. Whether it's a photo album from your latest vacation or an important document for work, sharing is as simple as sending a link to your friends, family, or colleagues. They can then view, edit, or comment on your files, based on the permissions you set.

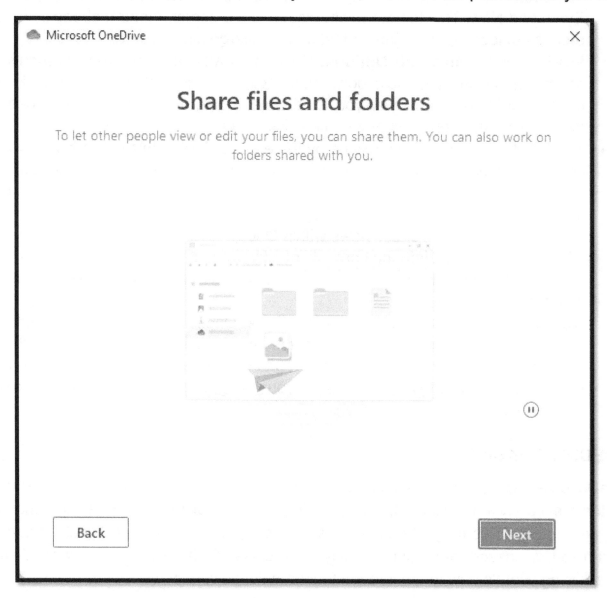

5. **Syncing Across Devices:** OneDrive seamlessly syncs your files across all your devices. This means the changes you make to a document on your laptop will automatically update on your phone and tablet. It's like having your files follow you, always up- dated and accessible.

6. **Finding Files Quickly:** With OneDrive, you're equipped with powerful search tools. Can't remember where you saved that report? Just type in a keyword, and OneDrive will scout through your files to find it for you. It's like having a personal assistant dedicated to keeping your files in order.

7. **Using OneDrive with Microsoft Office**: OneDrive and Micros oft Office work hand in hand. You can start a new Word docu-ment or Excel spreadsheet right from OneDrive, and it'll be saved automatically. It's perfect for when inspiration strikes, and you're not near your usual workstation.
8. **Accessing Files Offline:** OneDrive also lets you access your files even when not having an internet connection. By marking files or folders for offline use, you can keep working regardless of your connection status. It's like packing essentials in your back- pack for a journey off the grid.
9. **Protecting Your Files:** Security is a top priority in OneDrive. With features like Personal Vault, you can add an extra layer of protection to your most sensitive files. It's akin to having a digital lockbox within your magic box.

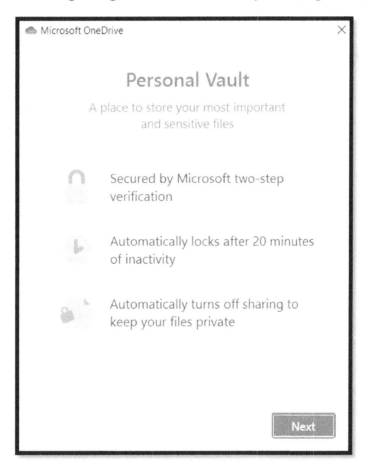

10. **Recovering Lost Files:** Ever deleted something by accident? OneDrive has your back with features like version history and the recycle bin. You can recover lost files or revert to earlier versions with just a few clicks. It's like having a time machine for your digital life.
11. **Customizing Your Experience:** One Drive allows for a level of customization that makes managing your digital files convenient and enjoyable. From choosing how files are displayed to setting up photo albums, your OneDrive can be as unique as you are.
12. **Integrating with Other Apps**: OneDrive doesn't stand alone; it plays we U with many other apps. Whether it's photo editing software or note-taking apps,

OneDrive can be the bridge that connects your files across services. It's like having all your tools talking to each other, streamlining your workflow.

13. **Staying Informed:** With OneDrive, you're never in the dark about what's happening with your files. Notifications keep you updated on changes, shares, and comments, ensuring you're always in the loop. It's like having a radar for your digital content.

14. **Exploring Advanced Features:** Beyond the basics, OneDrive offers a suite of advanced features for those looking to get even more out of their cloud storage. From setting expiration dates on shared links to automating work flows with Microsoft Power Autom ate, there's always something new to discover.

Some Signs on OneDrive and Their Meanings

You must have seen some signs or symbols on your OneDrive, but you do not know what they mean or what they stand for. In this part of my teaching, I will have the photos of these signs and inform you what they stand for. I have been using OneDrive for over 11 years and have seen some signs on the OneDrive main icon.

Two Rotate Signs on OneDrive

When you see the sign above on your OneDrive account, it means that a file you uploaded on your OneDrive is uploading to Mi-crosoft cloud. So, you must wait until that sign clears and see only the OneDrive icon. By waiting, I mean your computer should be connected to the internet until the file is uploaded fully.

Grey OneDrive icon

The grey OneDrive icon appearing in taskbar implies that the user has not signed in or the OneDrive setup did not complete.

Pause Symbol Over OneDrive Icon

When you see the sign above your OneDrive icon, it means your OneDrive is not syncing. Sometimes, you can see the above pause sign over the main OneDrive icon. There may be a reason for that. It can be because the Wi-Fi you are connected to is metered. As a result, it is configured so that OneDrive cannot sync using the data of the Wi-Fi. Also, the pause sign can be because your computer battery has gone down and automatically turned to battery-saving mode. When the battery is in this mode, OneDrive is paused to sync automatically, irrespective of the fact that the computer is connected to the internet. As a user of OneDrive, you can put your OneDrive in pause mode. I have done that before. Sometimes, users do that because they are connected to the internet with their mobile data. As a result, they do not want to be charged more data from their mobile data. If you want to pause your OneDrive desk- top app and, in return, have the pause sign on it, these are the steps you need to take: Right-click the OneDrive icon on the taskbar of your computer. This action will display some options. The options are displayed in the photo below.

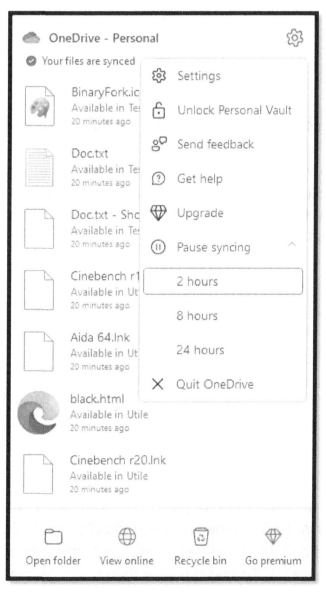

From the options you see when you right-click the icon, select Pause syncing, followed by how long you want the software paused. And immediately after that is done, you will see the pause sign appear over the OneDrive icon. It implies that the OneDrive software cannot upload any file on Microsoft cloud in that state. Everything is put on pause. But what if you want the software to start sync-ing files again? It is possible to bring OneDrive software back to its working mode. And for you to do that, you need to right-click the OneDrive icon on your computer's taskbar. This will display some options. Just click the pause mode for it to be disabled.

You can also click Resume syncing for it to be out of the pause mode. These are all on the pause over the OneDrive icon.

Warning on OneDrive Icon

When you see this icon on your OneDrive icon, it does not tell something good. Any time you see that warning triangle on your OneDrive account or the OneDrive icon, your attention is needed on your OneDrive account. So, click that sign as it appears on the icon to see the next action you must take to resolve the issue. In the end, the challenge will be fixed. But know that your computer must be connected to the internet for any action you want to take to be successful.

Red Circle withs lant Crossed Lines

That sign above does not commonly appear on the OneDrive icon in your computer's taskbar section. But in general, it can appear. For example, it can appear on the file you uploaded to the OneDrive folder. When you see the sign, it implies that a folder or file in your OneDrive account cannot be synced. In addition, this can appear when you delete a file or folder from OneDrive. To find out how the challenge may be resolved, click the notification, and follow the guide you are given.

No Entry Sign on OneDrive

This sign may appear on your OneDrive icon, which you need to understand. When you see that sign over your OneDrive icon, Microsoft has blocked your OneDrive account. Again, you can appeal by contacting OneDrive to see if the issue may be resolved, and you then have your account back.

People icon appearing beside a file or folder

This means the file with the people icon beside it has been shared with others.

The Blue Cloud icon

If this icon should appear next to a folder or file on OneDrive, it simply means that the file cannot be accessed offline.

Green tick icon

This indicates that an online-only file has been downloaded to your device and is now accessible without the internet.

The green circle with a white checkmark

This indicates that files will always keep on your device even when your free up space. They are always available offline on your device.

Padlock icon

The padlock icon appearing next to sync status means that the folder or file has settings that do not approve syncing.

The Flashing OneDrive icon

This is common in Android phones. It appears briefly as a normal part of the uploading process.

Three little blue lines

They appear like glimmer marks on a file or a folder, meaning that the file or folder is new.

Available edit OneDrive options

To edit a document on OneDrive, first sign in with your Microsoft account. Enter your e-mail address and password. Once you have signed in, you will be taken to the OneDrive web application, where you can edit your document. Once logged in, you can click on the document and edit it, as necessary.

The OneDrive cloud icon will appear on your Menu bar. Click on it to open the Preferences window. From here, choose Files On- Demand. You can select "Download files as you need" or "Download all files at once." You can also mark items as offline or online only in Finder.

WHAT ARE THE PLANS FOR ONEDRIVE?

OneDrive is a cloud storage service that allows users to access various data from anywhere. The program offers file synchroniza-tion, tagging, and more. It also allows users to download specific files when needed. This is useful for people who have limited stor-age space. Users can also set up restrictions on their data and file access.

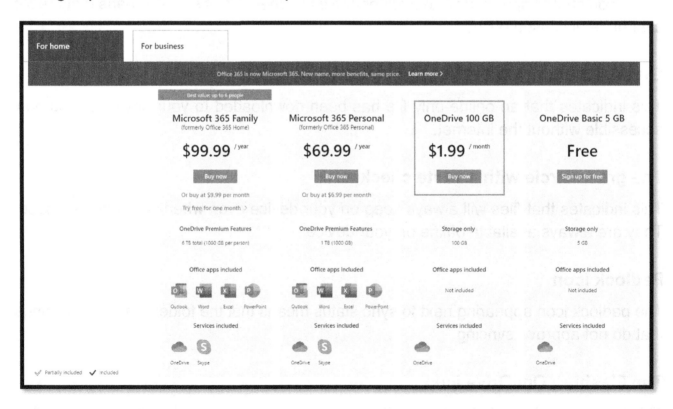

In June, Microsoft announced new storage plans for OneDrive. For those who subscribe to Office 365 One Drive storage will increase to 1 TB. This will cost $1.99 monthly, and users can change the plan anytime. Microsoft initially said these plans would be available in the coming months. However, today, the Microsoft Store has listed them. OneDrive is compatible with Microsoft Office 365, Outlook, and OneNote. It also offers e-mail support and is protected by two-factor authentication. However, OneDrive does not offer zero-knowledge encryption. However, users can enable in-transit AES 25 6-bit encryption for their files. For business users, OneDrive business plans offer greater benefits than personal plans. They offer unlimited storage, advanced security, and compli-ance features. However, unlike personal plans, business users can share files with others, so personal use plans aren't a good option if you're working alone. OneDrive for Business allows businesses to access files and collaborate on projects from anywhere. They can also share files and assign permissions. The service is a good replacement for the 'My Documents' folder on a local computer. For only $10 per month, business users can get unlimited storage for their files. Additionally, they can eliminate the risk of data corrup-tion due to hardware failure.

Microsoft has added various features to OneDrive, including creating and editing files on demand. In addition, OneDrive is also privacy-conscious, offering various sharing options. Users can choose whether to keep their files in the cloud or locally. Microsoft OneDrive also offers business plans for businesses, with features including file auditing and user management. Plans one and two cost$5 per user per month but do not include Microsoft 365 apps. Business Plan 2 gives business users unlimited individual cloud storage and advanced security.

CHAPTER 4: SYNCING YOUR FILES

Synchronization is more than just a technical process; it's a bridge that links your work, ideas, and projects across various platforms and devices. Imagine typing a document on your desktop at work, and by the time you reach home and open your laptop, the docu-ment is there, updated and waiting for you. That's synchronization at its core- a facilitator of modern productivity and flexibility. The journey of understanding synchronization begins with recognizing its pivotal role in our digital interactions. It ensures that the latest version of your document, photo, or project is accessible wherever you are, eliminating the need for cumbersome physical storage devices or the fear of working on out dated versions. But how does synchronization work under the hood? It involves a series of steps where changes made in one location are mirrored across all other locations where your OneDrive account is active. This process is continuous, ensuring real-time updates and backups.

OneDrive's synchronization isn't just about convenience; it's a safeguard for your digital content. It ensures that your files are not just stored but also protected and easily recoverable, giving you peace of mind in the fast-paced digital world.

What is synchronization?

Synchronization is a term that describes one of two concepts: the synchronization of processes and data. While the two are closely related, they are not the same.

Synchronization in OneDrive is like magic. It's a process that makes sure the files you work on from one device show upon all your other devices. This means if you start a document on your computer at home, you can finish it on your tablet at a coffee shop.

Synchronization, or 'sync' for short, is when your files update across all your devices automatically. It's like when you save a game on your console, and you can pick up where you left off on your friend's console.

Synchronization helps organizations protect data against potential data breaches. Data leakage or breaches can harm a company's reputation and revenue. A synchronization tool keeps data safe and synchronized according to each system's security require-ments.

Why Synchronization Matters: Sync is crucial because it saves time and reduces mistakes. Without it, you might end up working on an old version of a file. Imagine drawing a picture, then coming back to find someone erased part of it. Sync keeps your drawing safe.

Starting the Sync Process: The first step in syncing is having OneDrive on your devices. When you save a file to OneDrive, it's like putting it in a special box. This box exists on all your devices where OneDrive is set up.

The Role of the Cloud: When you add a file to OneDrive, it first goes up to the cloud. Think of the cloud as a big, secure library in the sky. Your file is stored there, safe and sound.

Updating Your Devices: After your file is in the cloud, OneDrive sends it to your other devices. It's like having clones of your file that appear everywhere you need them. This way, no matter where you are, your file is the same.

What Happens When You Make Changes: Every time you change a file, OneDrive repeats this process. It updates the file in the cloud, then updates the file on all your devices. It ensures you're always working with the latest version.

Benefits of Staying in Sync: With synchronization, you don't have to worry about losing your work or dealing with outdated files. It's like having a personal assistant who keeps everything organized for you.

Working Offline: Sometimes, you might not have the internet. With OneDrive, you can still work on your files. The next time you connect to the internet, OneDrive will update your changes across your devices.

Collaboration Made Easy: Sync also makes it easy to work with others. You and your friends can work on the same project from different places. It's like being in the same room, even if you're miles apart.

Keeping Your Files Safe: Besides keeping your files up-to-date, synchronization also keeps them safe. If something happens to your device, your files are still safe in the cloud. It's like having a backup plan for your digital life.

OneDrive Selective Sync: lets you choose which files to sync. This way, you can save space on your devices by only syncing what you need. It's like picking your favorite books to put on a shelf and storing the rest in the attic.

Troubleshooting Sync Issues: Sometimes, sync might not work perfectly. When this happens, OneDrive helps you fix the problem. It's like having a toolbox for your digital files.

Understanding Sync Status: OneDrive shows you if your files are synced. This way, you always know if your files are up to date. It's like having a traffic light for your digital work.

Security in Sync: OneDrive keeps your files secure during sync. It's like locking your files in a vault while they travel across the internet.

The Power of the Latest Version: Sync ensures you always have the latest version of your files. It's like always hav-ing the newest edition of your favorite book.

HOW TO SYNCHRONIZE FILES

To synchronize your files across devices using Microsoft OneDrive, follow these straightforward steps:

1. **Install OneDrive:** Download and install the OneDrive app on all devices you want to synchronize. This includes PCs, Macs, smartphones, and tablets.
2. **Sign In:** Open OneDrive on each device and sign in with your Microsoft account. Use the same account on all devices to ensure synchronization.

Microsoft OneDrive   ✕

Your OneDrive folder

Add files to your OneDrive folder so you can access them from other devices and still
have them on this PC.

Your OneDrive folder is here

C:\Users\JP\OneDrive

Change location

[Next]

Microsoft OneDrive   ✕

Back up your folders

Selected folders will sync in OneDrive - Personal. New and existing files will be added to
OneDrive, backed up, and available on your other devices even if you lose this PC. Learn
more.

Desktop	Documents	Pictures
0 KB	186 MB	1 KB

Space left in OneDrive after selection: 30.1 GB

[Continue]

3. **Choose Folders to Sync (on PC or Mac):** On your computer, right-click the OneDrive icon in the system tray or menu bar. Go to Settings > Account > Choose folders. Select the folders you want to sync and click OK.

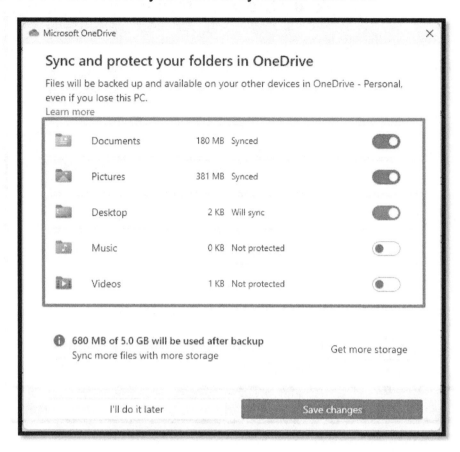

4. **Upload Files:** Drag and drop files or folders into the OneDrive folder on the computer or use the app to upload files on mobile devices. These will automatically sync across all devices logged into your account.
5. **Access Files on Another Device:** Open OneDrive on another device where you're signed in. You'll see the files you uploaded from the other device.
6. **Make Edits:** Any changes you make to a file on one device will automatically sync and update across all devices.
7. b If you edit files offline, they'll sync and update across your devices once you reconnect to the internet.
8. **Check Sync Status:** Look for sync status indicators on your files or folders. A green check mark means a file is synced, while a blue cloud icon means it's available online but not downloaded.
9. **Resolve Conflicts:** If you edit a file on two devices at the same time, OneDrive may create a second version. You can choose which version to keep.
10. **Use OneDrive Online:** You can also access and edit files directly from the OneDrive website, and changes will sync across all devices.

TROUBLESHOOTING SYNCHRONIZATION ISSUES

When you use OneDrive to keep your files in sync, sometimes things don't go as planned.

Here's how to fix common problems so your files stay up to date on all your devices.

1. Check Your Internet Connection

First, make sure you're connected to the internet. Sync needs a good connection to work. If you're offline, get online and see if that fixes the issue.

2. Look for the OneDrive Icon

On your computer, find the OneDrive cloud icon. It's usually at the bottom right. This icon tells you what's happening with your sync.

3. Pause and Res tart Sync

Sometimes, pausing OneDrive sync and starting it again can fix problems. Right-click the OneDrive icon and hit pause. Wait a bit, then restart it.

4. Update OneDrive

Make sure your OneDrive app is up to date. An old version might not work right. Goto the app store on your device to check for updates.

5. Check Your Storage

If OneDrive is full, it can't sync anymore. Check how much space you have. You might need to delete some things or get more storage.

6. Reset OneDrive

If nothing else works, you can reset OneDrive. But be careful, this makes OneDrive start syncing all over again. On a PC, you can reset by running a simple command. Look up how to do it for your device.

7. Check File Names

OneDrive doesn't like certain characters in filenames. Make sure your file names don't have symbols like"•: < >?/ \ I. Also, files can't be too big. Keep them under the size limit.

8. Make Sure You're Signed In

If you're not signed into OneDrive with the right account, it won't sync. Check which accounts you're using, especially if you have more than one.

9. Use the Website

If a file won't sync, try uploading it on the OneDrive website. This can sometimes get around problems.

10.   Check for Conflicting Files

If two files have the same name or are open at the same time on different devices, it can cause issues. Close the files or make sure their names are different.

11.   Check Your Device's Sync Settings

On phones and tablets, OneDrive might not sync in the background. Check your device's settings to make sure OneDrive is allowed to run all the time.

12.   Look at the Sync Errors

OneDrive will tell you if there are sync errors. Click or tap the OneDrive icon to see what the errors are and get tips on how to fix them.

13.   Rein stall OneDrive

As a last resort, you can uninstall and then reinstall OneDrive. This is like starting fresh and can often fix syncing issues.

14.   Contact Support

If you've tried everything and still have problems, it might be time to contact Microsoft support. They can help solve tricky issues.

SYNC BEST PRACTICES - TIPS FOR EFFICIENT SYNCHRONIZATION

When you're using OneDrive to keep your files synchronized across multiple devices, efficiency is key. Here are some best practices to ensure your synchronization process is as smooth as possible, without overloading your internet connection.

Understand What Synchronization Means

Synchronization with OneDrive means keeping your files and folders the same across your devices and the cloud. When you change a file on one device, it updates everywhere.

Use a Stable Internet Connection

A stable and reliable internet connection is crucial for effective sync. If your connection is slow or keeps dropping, files may not sync properly.

Manage Bandwidth Settings

OneDrive allows you to manage how much of your internet connection it uses. You can limit the upload and download rates, so syncing doesn't slow down your other online activities.

Prioritize Your Files

Not everything needs to be synced immediately. Prioritize files you need across devices.

Other, less important files can wait.

Use Selective Sync

Selective Sync lets you choose which folders to sync to your device. This saves space on your device and reduces the amount of data needing synchronization.

Check the File Size and Type

Large files take longer to sync. If possible, compress them. Also, some file types might not sync, like temporary or system files. Check which files are supported.

Keep Your OneDrive Updated

Using the latest version of OneDrive ensures you have the newest features and bugfixes. This can make synchronization more efficient.

Monitor Your Sync Status

Keep an eye on the OneDrive sync status to catch any issues early. If there's a problem, you'll see a notification explaining the issue and how to fix it.

Avoid Editing Files Simultaneously on Different Devices

When you open and edit a file on two devices at the same time, it can create conflicting copies. Try to work on files from one device at a time.

Use Files On-Demand

Files On-Demand is a feature that shows all your files in OneDrive without having to download them all. This saves space and band- width because you only download what you need.

Schedule Large Sync s for Off-Peak Hours

If you have a lot of data to sync, do it during off-peak hours when your internet connection is not heavily used. This can speed up the sync process.

Ensure Your Device's Date and Time Settings Are Correct

Incorrect date and time on your device can cause sync issues. Make sure they are set correctly.

Restart OneDrive to Reset Sync

If the sync seems stuck, try restarting OneDrive. Right-click the OneDrive icon, click

"Close OneDrive," and open it again.

Keep an Eye on Your Storage Limit

If you're nearing your storage limit in OneDrive, files might not sync. Check your storage and free up space or consider purchasing additional storage.

Organize Your Files

Well-organized files and folders make it easier to manage what you're syncing. Use clear, descriptive names for your folders and files.

Regularly Check for Errors

OneDrive will notify you of any sync errors. Address these promptly to ensure everything stays up to date.

Stay Informed About New Features

Microsoft regularly updates OneDrive. New features can improve synchronization. Keep up with the latest OneDrive news and updates.

Use a Wired Connection for Initial Syncs

If you're syncing a large amount of data for the first time, consider using a wired internet connection. It's usually faster and more stable than Wi-Fi.

Review Shared File Settings

If you're collaborating on shared files, review the settings to ensure everyone has the appropriate access and that shared files sync correctly.

CHAPTER 5: ONEDRIVE VS. COMPETITORS

Comparing OneDrive to its competitors involves looking at several key aspects: storage capacity and pricing, security features, ease of use, and unique functionalities. For instance, Google Drive offers Google Photos, a powerful tool for managing images. Dropbox stands out with its block-level file transfer algorithms, making file syncing faster. Meanwhile, Apple's iCloud Drive provides a smooth experience for users deeply embedded in the Apple ecosystem, offering convenient integration across macOS, iOS, and iPad OS devices. This chapter explores the differences, providing a comprehensive comparison that helps you understand where OneDrive shines and where it might fall short. We'll explore how it fares against giants like Google Drive, Dropbox, and iCloud.

Whether you're a student, a professional, or just looking to back up your family photos and videos, understanding these nuances will empower you to make an informed decision about which cloud storage service best meets your needs.

OneDrive vs. Google Drive

Microsoft OneDrive is a cloud storage program similar to Google Drive. However, its features are limited compared to those of Google. For example, you can no longer collaborate in real-time on your Google Drive documents and must give everyone permis-sion to edit your work. Also, OneDrive's search engine is not as effective as Google's.

The cost of using OneDrive is slightly lower than Google's. One Drive offers two types of plans, one for free and one for a small fee. Google Drive has a free tier that allows you to upload up to 15GBof files. However, you have to pay a monthly subscription to access unlimited space. Unlike Google Drive, Microsoft OneDrive has no limit on how many files you can store, and you can upgrade at any time without worrying about your storage limit.

OneDrive also has an app that allows you to work offline. The app will enable you to sync your files with multiple devices. It can also be accessed through the web. Both programs allow you to create folders and store files. They are both compatible with many file formats. They also provide you with access to other applications and hardware. Microsoft OneDrive is a cloud storage option that allows you to store personal information and exchange files. It is similar to Google Drive, but Microsoft OneDrive offers more storage space. OneDrive is great for projects that involve large amounts of files. To use OneDrive, you must sign up fora Microsoft account and download the desktop and mobile apps. The files sync automatically across all your devices without interruption.

Another essential aspect to consider when comparing Google Drive vs. OneDrive is security. The higher the security, the less likely a data leak or account compromise will occur. However, there is no 100 percent security guarantee when using a public cloud storage service, so you must trust the service provider. Microsoft OneDrive is a cloud storage service that integrates well with Microsoft apps and integrates easily. It also syncs information between accounts, making sharing files with other users easier. However, Google Drive is widely used, and its free version is very generous. Both options are useful for file sharing and collaboration.

OneDrive vs. SharePoint

OneDrive and SharePoint are widely used document management systems, but their functionality differs. While SharePoint helps businesses improve their workflow and ensure regulatory compliance, OneDrive suits individuals and personal users more. Read on to learn more about the differences between these two cloud storage services. And keep reading for a comprehensive OneDrive vs. SharePoint comparison. You'll be glad you did! Here's how to choose the right one for your needs!

Both services offer centralized storage for personal and work-related files. SharePoint allows users to share files with multiple peo-ple, while OneDrive will enable users to edit data only if they have administrator permissions. This feature is ideal for storing first drafts and other personal files that others won't access. OneDrive is ideal for individuals who want to store documents in a secure online folder. However, it is not ideal for business users, as it's not designed for sharing with external users. In addition, OneDrive users are limited to 1TB of storage, which limits its ability to be used for projects in a business setting. However, users can pay for additional storage to increase their storage capacity. SharePoint can handle up to 15TBof data.

SharePoint is a more effective tool for collaboration than OneDrive, allowing entire offices to create online workspaces. With SharePoint, users can manage their projects through calendars, status updates, and deadline notifications. However, One Drive and SharePoint also offer some unique features, making them distinctly different. For example, OneDrive is primarily used to share pri-vate files, while SharePoint is a hub for collaborative work.

SharePoint is a cloud-based storage service designed to allow teams to collaborate. OneDrive is best for personal use, while Share- Point is a popular cloud-based solution for business use. For personal use, OneDrive is better if you use Office or Windows for your business. In addition to sharing files, OneDrive also offers co-authoring and version history. OneDrive supports mobile devices and syncing files across the internet.

Microsoft OneDrive is cheaper than SharePoint. SharePoint online costs $5 per user per month for individual users and $10 per user per month for a small enterprise. For larger businesses, SharePoint is included in the Office 365 E3 suite, which costs $20 per user. OneDrive starts at a basic plan of 5 GB for individual users. Two plans are also available for businesses, and OneDrive for Business costs $5 per user per month.

OneDrive vs. Dropbox

Microsoft's OneDrive offers a much more flexible subscription plan. For example, for $10 a month, you can get unlimited photo storage. OneDrive also provides an impressive list of apps and is part of Microsoft 's Office 365 suite. If you want to share large files, both services offer flexible sharing options, including the ability to add an expiration date. OneDrive provides a synchronized file system that you can access from any computer. It also allows for secure file transfer and version history. For added security, it also offers archival recovery and password protection. It is also easy to use. OneDrive is particularly useful for businesses and students who need a convenient cloud storage service. The primary differences between OneDrive and Dropbox are their storage capacity and features. Dropbox is free for individuals, while OneDrive is a paid service. Businesses can get unlimited space by paying a monthly subscription. Dropbox 's free plan only offers 500 GB of space. Depending on the size of your files, you may need to pay more for storage space. If you're looking for a cloud storage option for your organization, OneDrive is the better choice. OneDrive is more secure than Dropbox. Both services use AES 25 6-bit encryption to keep your files safe and secure. OneDrive's encryption is effective both in in-transit and at rest. Both Dropbox and OneDrive also offer two-factor authentication to protect your files.

Whether you're storing your files in the cloud or on your device, encryption is the key to protecting your data. Dropbox is a pop-ular cloud storage service and has over 200 million users. Its simple interface makes sharing files snap. Dropbox also includes a collaborative document tool called Dropbox Paper. While Dropbox Paper isn't a replacement for native office apps, it does offer an additional security layer. Dropbox offers a rewind feature, allowing users to restore a previous file version. Unlike Google Drive, however, Drop box has a limit of 30 days on which you can restore a file. Drop box does not have an e-mail client or office suite, but it does offer other features, such as a note-taking app, document signer, file transfer service, and a password manager. Dropbox also lets you take screenshots.

OneDrive vs. iCloud

OneDrive is a cloud storage service that comes pre-installed on Windows and Mac computers. Users can sign in and access files stored in OneDrive by using their user accounts. This makes the service an excellent choice for both personal and business use. OneDrive also offers the added benefit of being convenient and cost-effective. While iCloud works better for users of Apple devices, OneDrive is designed to work with any device. It has more options for mobile use than iCloud and comes with a generous five-gi-gabyte free storage plan. You can also pay for up to one terabyte of storage for a fee. Despite its simplicity, OneDrive is not without its drawbacks. While the OneDrive app is convenient, it lacks zero-knowledge encryption, so Microsoft can share your encryption keys with third-party providers and authorities. However, if you use OneDrive, you will be notified of any data breach as soon as possible. You can then change your password and turn on additional security features. Microsoft OneDrive has several downsides over iCloud, but if you're an Apple user, iCloud is the better choice.

If you own an iPhone or Mac, you can easily activate iCloud on all your devices. Your back-ups are instantly synchronized with all your Apple devices, and your files are accessible from any device. However, iCloud is more convenient for iPhone and Apple users because it's compatible with Windows devices. When it comes to security, iCloud is superior to OneDrive. It offers two-factor au-thentication and encryption, but you must pay to enable it. This makes it much harder for unauthorized users to access your files. You must back up your data regularly with these two cloud storage services.

In general, OneDrive and iCloud both offer solid cloud storage solutions. However, you should choose based on your personal needs. For example, if you don't own an iPhone or an iPad, you may find OneDrive a better choice.

Summary of the Comparison

When comparing OneDrive to other cloud storage applications, it's beneficial to breakdown the comparison into specific subtopics: Integration, Storage and Pricing, Security Features, and User Experience. This structured approach allows us to understand the dis- tinct advantages and limitations of OneDrive in contrast to its competitors.

Integration

- **OneDrive** offers seamless integration with Windows and Microsoft Office, making it an ideal choice for users heavily invested in Microsoft products.
- **Google Drive** integrates closely with Google Workspace (formerly G Suite), appealing to users who prefer Google's ecosystem for collaboration and productivity.
- **Dropbox** focuses on wide compatibility, offering integrations with numerous third-party apps and services, making it versatile for users with diverse needs.
- **Apple iCloud** is deeply integrated with iOS and macOS, offering a streamlined experience for Apple device users, though it's less flexible for non-Apple environments.

Storage and Pricing

- **OneDrive** provides a range of plans, including free storage and additional space with Office 365 subscriptions, offering value for money, especially for Office users.
- **Google Drive** offers generous storage options with Google One plan s, appealing due to its expansive storage at competitive prices.

- **Dropbox** offers various tiers, including Dropbox Plus and Professional, known for its high storage limits but at a higher cost compared to others.
- **Apple iCloud** provides several storage tiers but tends to be more expensive for the storage provided, especially beyond the basic plan.

Security Features

- **OneDrive** has robust security measures, including two-factor authentication, ransomware detection, and file recovery, ensur-ing user data protection.
- **Google Drive** also offers strong security features, including two-factor authentication and encryption, making it a secure op-tion for personal and professional use.
- **Dropbox** emphasizes security with two-factor authentication, SSL/ T LS encryption, and has introduced features like Dropbox Vault for sensitive files.
- **Apple iCloud** use send-to-end encryption for certain data types and two-factor authentication, focusing on maintaining user privacy and security.

User Experience

- **OneDrive** is known for its clean interface and deep integration with Windows, providing a native and intuitive user experience for Windows users.
- **Google Drive** offers a straightforward, user-friendly interface that integrates well with other Google services, appealing to users familiar with the Google ecosystem.
- **Dropbox** features a simple, intuitive design and reliable file syncing, making it user-friendly, though it may lack the depth of integration seen in OneDrive and Google Drive.
- **Apple iCloud** offers a seamless experience on Apple devices, with a focus on simplicity and integration, though it may be less intuitive for users on non-Apple platforms.

GUIDELINES TO CHOOSING THE RIGHT SERVICE FOR YOU

When choosing the right cloud storage service for your needs, there are several key factors to consider. These factors help ensure that you select a service that not only meets your current requirements but is also scalable for future needs. Here's a guide to help you make an informed decision:

1. Storage Capacity

Determine how much storage space you need. OneDrive, for example, offers various plans with different storage capacities, starting from the free plan with limited storage to premium plans with extensive storage options. Assess your current data volume and po-tential growth to choose a plan that accommodates your files without unnecessary expenses.

2. Security Features

Security is paramount when it comes to cloud storage. OneDrive provides robust security features, including two-factor authenti-cation, ransomware detection, and file recovery options. Compare these features with those of competitors like Google Drive, Drop- box, and iCloud to understand which service offers the level of security you require. Consider whether the service offers encryption for data at rest and in transit, as well as the company's privacy policy and compliance with regulations like GDPR.

3. Pricing and Plans

Analyze the cost-effectiveness of each plan. OneDrive integrates seamlessly with Microsoft 365 subscriptions, adding value for users already within the Microsoft ecosystem. Compare subscription plans across different services, looking at not just the cost but also the benefits included, such as the amount of storage, access to office suites, and any additional features like advanced security or business collaboration tools.

4. Accessibility and Ease of Use

Consider the platform's user interface and accessibility. OneDrive is known for its integration with Windows and Microsoft prod-ucts, making it a convenient option for users heavily invested in Microsoft 's ecosystem. Evaluate how each cloud service integrates with your devices and workflow. Ease of use, mobile app availability, and integration with third-party apps are important factors to consider.

5. Collaboration Features

If you work in a team or share files frequently, look for services that offer robust collaboration tools. OneDrive, for instance, allows real-time collaboration on documents within the Microsoft suite. Compare such features across services to find one that best sup- ports your collaboration needs, including file-sharing controls, simultaneous editing capabilities, and integration with communi-cation tools.

6. Bandwidth and Speed

Check the service's performance, especially if you frequently upload or download large files. Some services may limit bandwidth or have slower speeds on certain plans. Consider testing the upload and download speeds of the services you're interested in to ensure they meet your requirements.

7. Customer Support and Reliability

Research each service's reliability and customer support. Look for reviews and testimonials regarding uptime, data loss incidents, and how the company handles customer issues. Support options, including live chat, email, and phone support, can be crucial in ur-gent situations.

8. Data Recovery and Versioning

Consider how each service handles data recovery and file versioning. OneDrive offers version history for documents, which can be invaluable for recovering from accidental deletions or unwanted changes. Ensure the cloud storage you choose has a straight forward process for recovering your data when needed.

Choosing the right cloud storage service involves balancing these factors based on your personal or business needs. OneDrive stands out for users already utilizing Microsoft products, offering integrated services and security.

CHAPTER 6: EFFICIENT FILE MANAGEMENT

In our deep dive into mastering file management with Microsoft OneDrive, we unlock the secrets to keeping your digital life orga-nized and at your fingertips. Starting with the basics, we guide you through uploading your files seamlessly. Whether you're on your phone, tablet, or computer, getting your files into OneDrive is a breeze. But it doesn't stop there; we also cover organizing these files into folders, making sharing a piece of cake, and ensuring you can always find what you need with OneDrive's smart search features. Plus, we share tips on using version history to your advantage, ensuring you never lose an important change again. But OneDrive is more than just a place to store your files. It's a tool for collaboration and security. We'll walk you through sharing files with others, setting permissions to keep your information safe, and even collaborating in real-time on documents. With OneDrive, your files aren't just stored; they're active tools that help you work smarter, not harder.

CREATING NEW FOLDERS

- Select the option for New
- Select the folder from the drop-down menu

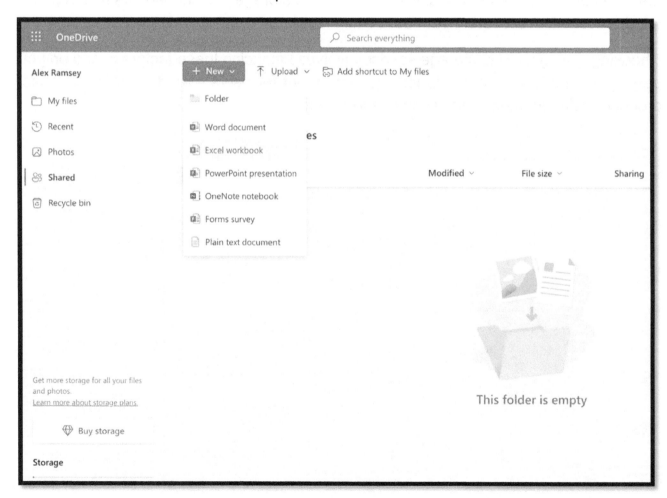

- Type in a name for the newly created folder and select Create

Opening documents on ONEDRIVE

- In the **Files** window, select the document to be opened, for instance, a PowerPoint file
- In the **Preview window** of the selected document, select the **Edit** drop-down opt io n
- Select **Edit** in a **Browser**

The document is then opened and can also be edited.

- Select OneDrive at the top of the opened document to close the document

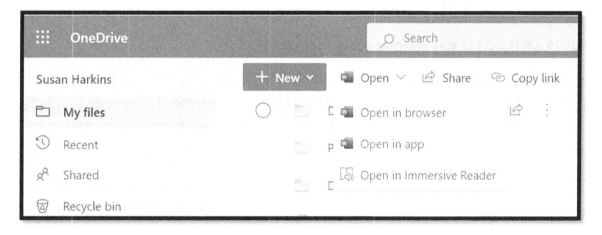

CREATING A FOLDER IN A FOLDER

Yes, creating a folder in an already created folder is possible. Let me assume that you are a book writer. As a writer, you first created a folder named "BOOKS." Inside that folder, you gave the name "Books," you have book files you published in different years. For example, you may have published books in 2013, 2014, 2015, 2016, 2018, 2019, 2020, and 2021. Irrespective of the fact that these books are inside one folder you named "BOOKS," you can decide to organize the books year by year. It means I need to create folders inside that "BOOKS" folder with names such as 2013, 2014, 2015, 2016, 2018, 2019, 2020, and 2021. All the books I published in 2013 will be inside the folder named

"2013".All 2014 books will be put inside the folder named "2014,"and soon. To create a folder in an already created folder, the first step you need to take after signing into your OneDrive account is to click My files tab and then click the parent folder where you want to create a new folder. Then, as that folder opens, click. When you click the **new** command, select a folder from the list of options. As that command is selected, type the name you want the folder to bear, followed by the **Cre- ate** command. That is all on how to create a folder in an already existing folder.

UPLOADING FILES TO ONEDRIVE

1. **Open OneDrive:** Start by opening the OneDrive app on your device or accessing OneDrive through a web browser.
2. **Choose Upload Method:**
- For desktop: Drag and drop files directly into your OneDrive folder.
- For mobile: Tap the"+" or upload icon and select the files from your device.
- Through a web browser: Click the "Upload" button and choose files or folders from your computer.
3. **Select File s or Folders:** Browse your device to find the files or folders you wish to upload.
4. **Confirm Upload:** After selecting, confirm the upload. The files will start uploading to your OneDrive cloud storage.

DOWNLOADING FILES FROM ONEDRIVE

Have you been in a place where you needed a document urgently? In that situation, since you did not have your personal computer to have that document, the only option left was to download that file from your OneDrive account and then print it from any cyber- cafe closest to you at that moment.

With OneDrive, you can download the document you saved there on your mobile phone or any computer and use it for what you want. I remember years back when I needed to submit my Curriculum Vitae (CV) to a company, which came unplanned. When I saw that opportunity, I did not have my personal computer. What I did was I looked for a nearby cybercafe and logged into my OneDrive account. From there, I could download the document and then print it out. I went ahead and submitted the file.

When you want to download any existing file in your OneDrive account, log into your OneDrive account. Next, click the **My files** tab to see all the files in your account. Next, locate the file you want to download and get it selected. And lastly, click the **Download** but- ton, which appears above the file.

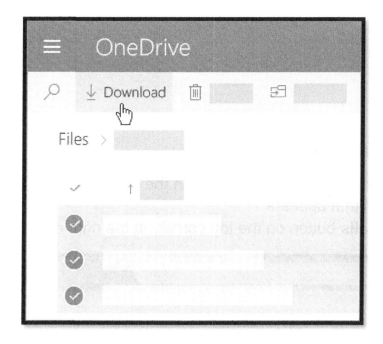

If you are downloading it on a computer, the system will ask you if you want to open the file or save it on your computer. In most cases, I choose the option to save it on my computer. Once the file is downloaded, you can find the file on your computer. If you have not changed the default section where files downloaded in your computer are saved, you will see the downloaded file in the down- load folder of your computer.

Opening Documents in OneDrive with the OneDrive Desktop Version

- Select the document to be opened and make a right-click
- Select the option to **Open the Document in PowerPoint**

Searching Files in OneDrive

1. **Access Your OneDrive:** Login to your OneDrive account through your web browser or open the OneDrive app on your device.
2. **Use the Search Box:** Locate the search box at the top of the page. In the OneDrive app, you might find it at the top or via search icon.
3. **Enter Your Search Query:** Type the name of the file or a keyword from the content you're looking for. OneDrive can search through file names, text within documents, and even text within images.
4. **Filter Your Search**: To narrow down your results, use the filter options. You can filter by file type (e.g., Word documents, PDFs), the date the file was last modified, or other available parameters.
5. **Select from the Results:** Browse through the search results to find the file you need. If your search returns too many items, try refining your query or using more specific keywords.

File and folder sharing in ONEDRIVE

- Find the folder or file. Set your cursor on the file or folder to be shared and select the **check** sign that appears
- Select the **Details** button on the top corner on the right of the screen

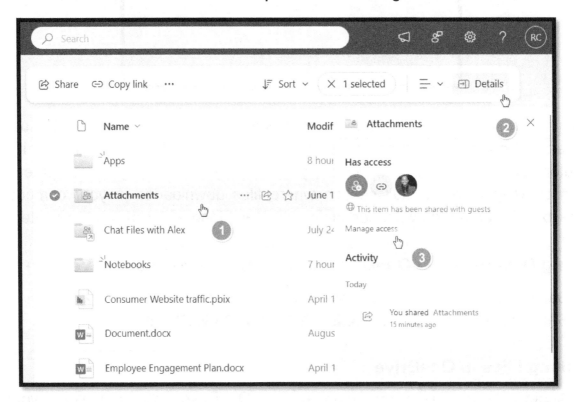

- Locate the **Sharing** menu. This might appear as an icon or a text link, depending on your view. Select the option for **Adding People**
- **Choose How to Share**: You'll have options to share directly with specific people, or to create a link that anyone can use. For di-rect sharing, enter the email addresses of the people you want to share with.
- In the resulting window, select either **Gene rate a Link** or select **E-mail**

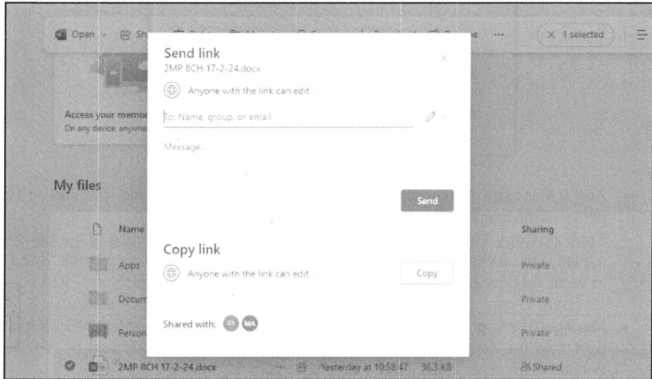

- **Set Permissions:** Decide whether recipients can edit the file or only view it. Toggle the permission settings according to your preference.

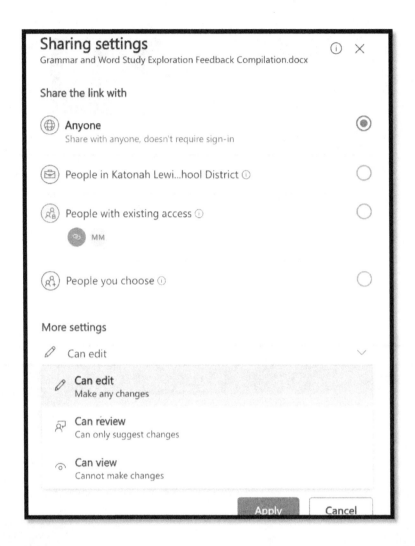

- **Add a Message (Optional):** If you're sharing directly with people, you can add a personal message to the email notification they'll receive.
- **Send or Copy Link:** If E-mail is chosen, enter the e-mail address of the person the file is to be shared with and then select Share. For direct sharing, click **"Send"** to email the invitation. If you're creating a link, choose whether to copy it to your clipboard to paste elsewhere, or to send via email directly from OneDrive.
- **Manage Sharing**: To review or change who has access to a shared file or folder, right-click the item and select "Manage access." Here you can add or remove people, change permissions, or stop sharing entirely.

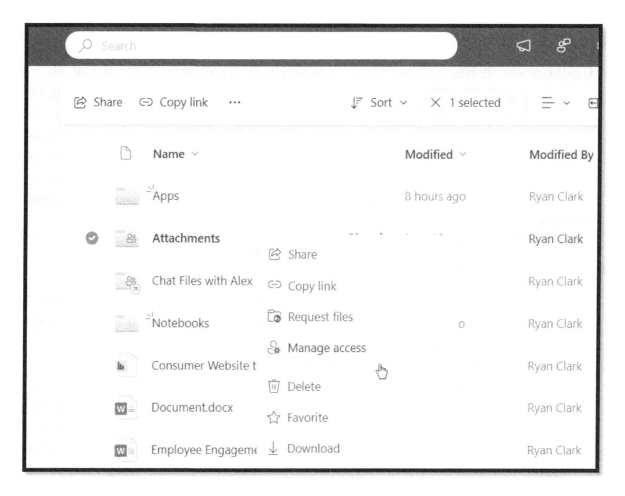

Depending on the permission granted to whom a file is shared, they can access and make changes to it at any time. In addition, they can edit and access the file if shared with multiple people. Whenever a person is working on a shared file, other scan seethe name of who is editing at the moment and a blinking cursor that shows the exact point the person is in the document.

Comments can also be written about shared documents. These comments are visible to all who have access to the document.

Enhancing Collaboration

1. **Collaborate in Real-Time:** Use OneDrive's integration with Microsoft 36 5 apps (like Word, Excel, and PowerPoint) to work on documents simultaneously with colleagues.
2. **Track Changes:** Make use of version history for shared documents to see who made changes and when. This is crucial for col-laboration on important projects.
3. **Review Shared Files:** Periodically review your shared files and folders to ensure that access permissions are up to date and that only the necessary people have access.

Organizing Files Efficiently in OneDrive

1. **Create Folders:** Right -cli ck (or tap and hold on mobile) in your OneDrive space and select "New Folder" to create a folder. Name it according to the category or project it will represent.
2. **Move Files into Folders:** Drag and drop files into these folders or use the move option by right-clicking on the file.
3. **Naming Files:** Use clear, descriptive names for your files and folders to make them easily searchable. Incorporate dates, project names, or specific descriptors.
4. **Use Tags and Descriptions**: If available, add tags and descriptions to your files for easier retrieval.

Advantages of Effective File Management

1. **Easy Access & Retrieval:** By organizing your files, you can quickly find what you need without sifting through clutter.
2. **Collaboration**: Share specific files or folders with colleagues or friends directly from OneDrive by right clicking the item and selecting "Share." You can set permissions to view or edit.
3. **Version Control**: Keep track of document versions automatically. Right -click on a file and select "Version history" to view or restore previous versions.
4. **Security & Backup:** With your files organized and uploaded to OneDrive, they are securely backed up in the cloud, protecting against data loss.

UNDERSTANDING VERSIONING AND FILE HISTORY

OneDrive automatically keeps versions of your files, allowing you to access and restore them to previous states. This feature is espe-cially useful if you've made changes to a document that you later decided weren't necessary or if you accidentally delete content.

1. **Accessing Version History:** To view a document's version history, right-click on the file in OneDrive and select "Version his-tory" from the context menu. This action will open a sidebar or a new window, depending on your access point (web or desktop app), listing all available versions of the document.

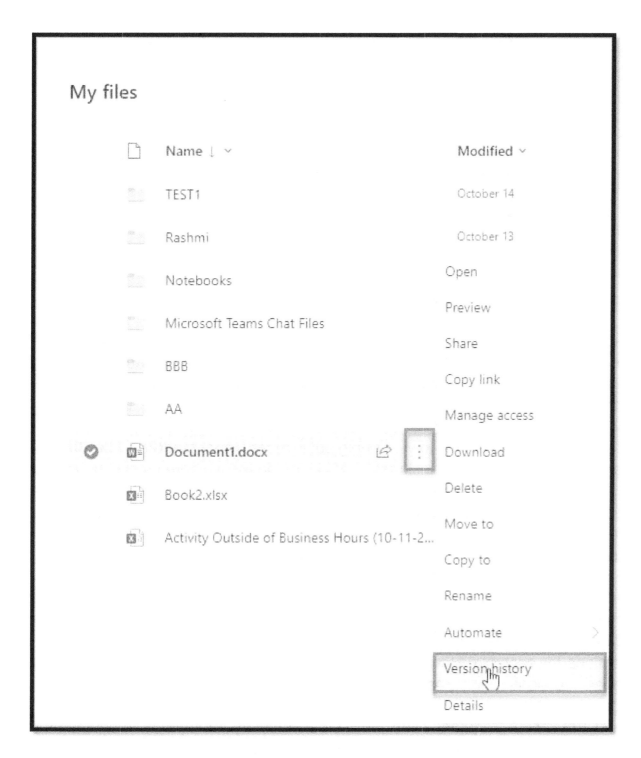

2. **Previewing Versions:** Before deciding which version to restore, you can preview each to ensure it's the correct one. Click on a version to see its details. Some versions might allow you to open and view the document directly, depending on the filetype.

Version History

Vers...	Modified Date	Modified
7.0	31m ago	Wendy Zu
6.0	41m ago	Wendy Zu
5.0	Wed at 1:59 PM	Wendy Zu
4.0	Tue at 5:13 PM	Wendy Zu
3.0	Tue at 5:12 PM	Wendy Zu
2.0	Tue at 5:09 PM	Wendy Zu

3. **Restoring a Previous Version: Once** you've found the version you want to revert to, look for the "Res t ore" option. Clicking this will replace the current version of the document with the one you've selected. Be mindful that this action is immediate, and while the replaced version will still be available in the version history, any unsaved changes in the current document will be lost.

4. File history works similarly to versioning but is more **Understanding File History:** comprehensive. It not only includes changes made to the contents of your files but also tracks renaming, moving, or deleting files. Accessing file history might require visiting the OneDrive recycle bin or exploring the "Activity" options for your files.

5. **Using the Recycle Bin:** If a file has been accidentally deleted, the OneDrive recycle bin is your first stop. Files remain here for a set period before being permanently removed. To restore a file, simply navigate to the recycle bin, select the file, and choose " Restore.11

6. **Managing Version Limits:** By default, OneDrive saves a certain number of versions for each file. However, for OneDrive for Business users, the number of saved versions might be higher or have customizable limits set by the administrator.

7. **Best Practices:** Regularly check your version history for important documents to familiarize yourself with the changes and updates made over time. This habit can be crucial for collaborative projects where multiple users edit the same document.

Remember, while OneDrive's versioning and file history features provide a safety net, maintaining good file management practices and regular backups of critical data is always recommended. This way, you ensure that your documents are safe and recoverable, even in unexpected situations.

CHAPTER 7: ENSURING SECURITY AND PRIVACY

One Drive 's approach to security and privacy encompasses several layers, including encryption both in transit and at rest. This means that whether your data is being uploaded to or stored on OneDrive, it's protected by robust encryption methods. Addition - ally, OneDrive offers t wo-factor authentication (2FA), adding an extra layer of security by requiring a second form of verification beyond just your password. Th is can significantly reduce the risk of unauthorized access, as an attacker would need both your pass- word and access to your second form of verification, like a mobile device.

Privacy settings in OneDrive allow users to control who can view or edit their files. By managing these settings, you can ensure that sensitive documents are shared only with those you trust. Furthermore, OneDrive's file history and versioning features are invalu-able tools for document management. They allow you to track changes and revert to earlier versions of a document if necessary, offering a safety net against accidental deletions or unwanted edits.

OneDrive also includes features designed to protect against ransomware, a type of malicious software that threatens to publish the victim's data or perpetually block access to it unless a ransom is paid. With OneDrive's recovery options, users can restore their files to a previous state before the attack occurred, mitigating the impact of such security threats.

UNDERSTANDING ONEDRIVE'S SECURITY FEATURES

When it comes to safeguarding your digital files on OneDrive, understanding its security features is paramount.

Encryption: The First Line of Defense

OneDrive uses encryption both when your data is at rest (stored on servers) and in transit (being uploaded or downloaded). This is like a digital lockbox, ensuring that only those with the correct key can access your information. Here's how it works step by step:

1. **Data Encryption:** As soon as you upload a file to OneDrive, it's encrypted, transforming it into a format that unauthorized users can't easily decipher.
2. **Secure Transmission:** When you access or transfer files, OneDrive uses Secure Socket Layer (SSL) encryption, creating a secure tunnel protected by digital certificates.

Two-Factor Authentication(2FA): An Extra Security Layer

Two-factor authentication adds a second security check to verify your identity, significantly enhancing your account's security. Implementing 2FA is simple:

1. **Activate 2FA:** Go to your Microsoft account settings and select the security options to turn on two-factor authentication.
2. **Verification Methods:** Choose a secondary verification method (phone call, text message, or app notification).
3. **Login Process**: After entering your password, you'll be prompted for a verification code from your chosen method, ensuring that only you can access your account.

Permission Settings: Controlling Access

OneDrive allows you to set permissions for your files and folders, giving you control over who can view or edit your data. Here's how to manage permissions:

1. **Select File/Folder:** Right-cli ck on the file or folder you want to share.
2. **Share Option:** Click on the 'Share ' option and choose who to share it with by entering their email addresses.
3. **Set Permissions:** Decide whether each person can edit or only view the file.

Regular Security Updates: Keeping Your Guard Up

Microsoft continuously releases security updates for OneDrive to protect against new threats. Ensure you're protected by:

1. **Automatic Updates:** Keep your OneDrive and Office applications set to update automatically.
2. **Stay Informed:** Occasionally check the official Microsoft Office and OneDrive blogs for news on updates or emerging threats.

Utilizing Advanced Security Measures

Beyond the basics, OneDrive offers advanced security options like Personal Vault for highly sensitive information, which requires a second step of identity verification to access.

PROTECTING YOUR DATA WITH ONEDRIVE

OneDrive's Approach to Data Safety

OneDrive ensures your files are not just stored but also protected. It's like a safe for your digital files. OneDrive keeps an eye out for dangers and warns you if it finds any. This means if something bad like ransomware tries to lock your files, OneDrive will alert you.

Here's how OneDrive keeps your data safe and how you can leverage its features for maximum security.

1. Stay Alert with Threat Monitoring (Setting up your defense)

OneDrive uses advanced Microsoft tools to continuously monitor for threats, ensuring your data is protected against potential risks.

Before any attack happens, OneDrive helps by watching for threats. This is your first defense line. It's crucial because it's easier to stop problems before they start.

- **Ransomware Detection:** OneDrive notifies Microsoft 365 users of any ransomware attacks, helping you respond quickly to threats.
- **Suspicious Activity Monitoring:** OneDrive looks out for signs of someone trying to get into your account without permission. It keeps an eye on your account 24/7foranyunauthorized access attempts, alerting you to suspicious activity as it happens. It's always on the lookout, ensuring no one sneaks in unnoticed.
- **Virus Scanning:** Downloaded documents are scanned for viruses using Windows Defender's anti-spam and anti-malware en-gines to identify harmful content.
2. Fortify Your First Line of Defense with Breach Prevention

OneDrive incorporates powerful Microsoft security features to strengthen your defense against cyber threats.

- **Encryption:** Your data is secured both in transit and at rest with advanced encryption technologies, ensuring only authorized users can access it.
- **Access Control:** Clearly define access permissions for your files and folders to control who can view or edit your data.
- **Password Protection:** Microsoft 36 5 users can set passwords for accessing files, adding an extra layer of security.
- **Expiring Links:** Share files with time-limited access by setting expiration dates for shared links.
- **OneDrive Personal Vault:** A special area within OneDrive that requires additional authentication, such as two-factor verifica-tion, for access. It offers enhanced protections like automatic locking and BitLocker encryption.
3. Establish a Safety Net with Data Recovery

While OneDrive has built-in data recovery tools, pairing these with a third-party backup solution is advised for complete data protection. Even with strong defenses, sometimes bad things happen. If your files get locked by ransomware (in case of a breach), OneDrive has tools to help you get them back.

- **Mass Deletion Alerts**: Receive immediate alerts with recovery steps if a large number of files are deleted. If many files get deleted at once, OneDrive will let you know. It'll even help you bring those files back.
- **Version History:** OneDrive keeps older versions of your files. Easily recover previous versions of files in case of accidental deletion or unwanted edits.
- **Ransomware Recovery:** For OneDrive for Business users, if ransomware attacks, you can undo the damage. OneDrive lets you roll back your entire drive to a time before the attack happened, up to 30 days after.

Optimal Cybersecurity Practices

For comprehensive protection, integrate OneDrive's security tools with the following best practices:

- **Strong Passwords:** Use complex passwords and change them regularly. Protect your OneDrive folder with a secure password.
- **Two-Factor Authentication(2FA):** Add an extra layer of security with 2FA, requiring a secondary code for account access.
- **Mobile Device Encryption:** Enable encryption on your devices to protect your files in the OneDrive app.
- **Regular Updates:** Keep your systems up to date with the latest security patches and enable auto-updates where possible. This helps fix security holes that hackers could use to get in.
- **Monitor Access Permissions**: Regularly review who has access to your data and adjust permissions as needed. Store sensitive information securely and limit access to confidential files.
- **Automation Tools:** Use the Office 365 admin Center to manage security settings and automate the identification and resolu-tion of security issues.

Remember:

While OneDrive offers many tools to protect and recover your data, it's also smart to use additional backup solutions. This way, you're extra safe and can recover your files even if OneDrive can 't help.

CHAPTER 8: EXPLORING ADVANCED FEATURES

OneDrive helps you work with others without being in the same room. You can share your work and make changes together. It's like having a team meeting, but online. This makes doing projects and homework a lot easier and more fun. Sometimes, you need to keep things safe, like a secret diary. OneDrive has special locks that keep your private stuff private. Only the people you choose can see your files. This is great for keeping your secrets safe. OneDrive can also talk to other Microsoft tools you use, like Word or Pow- er Point. This means you can start working on your computer and finish on your tablet without any problems. It's like having your work follow you around, ready whenever you are.

COLLABORATION TOOLS

OneDrive makes working together simple and efficient. Here's how you can use its tools to collaborate on documents in real-time with your team.

Sharing and Permissions

- **Share Easily:** Right-click on any document in OneDrive. Choose "Share" and select who to share it with. You can decide if they can view or edit.
- **Link Sharing:** Create a link for your document. Decide if the link allows editing or only viewing. This link can be sent to anyone, even if they don't have OneDrive.
- **Control Access:** You can stop sharing any file at any time. Just go to the file's details and click "Stop sharing."

Working Together

- **Edit Together:** Open a shared document. You'll see who else is working on it. You can see their changes as they type.
- **Comments and Ideas:** Use the comment feature to discuss changes. Tag team members to get their attention on specific parts of the document.

Permissions for Safety

- **Permission Levels:** Decide if someone can edit or only view your document. This keeps your files safe while letting others help.
- **Password Protection:** Add a password to sensitive documents. This means only people with the password can open it.

Finding Shared Files

- **Easy to Find:** Goto the "Shared" area in OneDrive. You'll see all the files others have shared with you. This makes it easy to keep track of teamwork.

Safe and Secure

- **Security First:** OneDrive keeps your shared files safe. It uses encryption, meaning only people you've shared with can see them.

Working together in real-time

With Microsoft 365, you can now work together on files in real time. File collaboration allows you to edit, comment, and share files with others. You can also easily see the changes that others make to your files and who made them. In addition, Microsoft OneDrive has collaboration functions for iOS and Android devices.

Collaborating online in real-time can benefit your team, even if you are not in the same Office. It allows everyone to view and com-ment on the same document, which helps you improve knowledge sharing. Many collaboration tools are available online, including desktop sharing, document sharing, and online whiteboards.

Microsoft Teams is another way to collaborate and share documents. The Teams app allows you to collaborate with your team members. For example, you can work on documents using a live chat application and share them with other team members. You can also use Microsoft Teams to share and edit files with others.

Microsoft 365 has many collaboration features, and OneDrive is a significant component. In addition to providing a collaborative environment, Microsoft 365 also provides features to help users keep their data secure. For example, you can control the amount of sharing, which can help you create a collaboration space and protect intellectual property.

Family Editing OneDrive document simultaneously

Using a Microsoft Account, you can share a file with more than one person. This way, several people can edit the same document simultaneously. Click the Share button on the document's list and check the box next to the file. This option is not available if you have a personal OneDrive account.

All group members need to be Microsoft OneDrive users to use group sharing. After the document is shared, you can set the permis-sions to allow other people to view and edit the file. You can also allow them to view and edit comments. In addition, you can create groups based on the people in your family.

Friends and Teammates

Microsoft OneDrive offers its users a great way to collaborate on documents. Users can create rich documents by adding files, YouTube videos, and social media posts. Once they're finished editing the documents, they can send them to other people. Users can even create groups to share their documents with others. This allows them to manage who has access to specific files and collabo- rate with them in real time.

Can users share and editdocuments on OneDrive?

OneDrive has a handy feature that allows people to share files and folders with other people. Once a recipient signs in with a Micro- soft account, they can view and edit the file. If recipients wish to change permissions, they can do so in the Sharing Options section.

You can share documents on OneDrive with any of your contacts. Theapp has a button on the right side that lets you select whom to share files and folders. To share files and folders with others, open the document, select Sharing, and then select the option to "Add People." You can also share files with e-mail addresses or social media.

If you want to share a document, you must have Microsoft Office on your computer. After you share the document, you can open it in the desktop Office application and edit it as if it were in the desktop Office program. The changes you make will be saved in OneDrive.

Once you've shared a document, you'll receive an e-mail notification from the recipient. You can enter their e-mail addresses in the e-mail address field or select their contact list. You can also select whether to give these people the right to edit the document. Alternatively, you can remove the sharing link.

Choosing the right setting for your document is very important. For example, in Microsoft OneDrive, users can limit the ability to share certain documents with specific people. The default setting is" Allow editing," but you can change this setting if you want to restrict access to the document.

INTEGRATING ONEDRIVE WITH MICROSOFT 36S

OneDrive and Microsoft 365 work together like a dream team. They make your work easy and keep everything in one place. Here's how you can use OneDrive with Office apps to get more done.

Working with Office Apps

OneDrive connects with Office apps like Word, Excel, and PowerPoint. You can save your files in OneDrive and open them in any Office app. No need to save them on your computer.

Sharing Made Simple

Sharing files is super easy with OneDrive and Microsoft 365. You can share a document from Word, for example, and choose who can see it and who can edit it. This makes working on projects with your team a breeze.

Always Up to Date

When you use OneDrive with Office apps, your files update in real time. If you change something in a document, everyone who has access can see the update right away.

Access from Anywhere

With OneDrive, you can get to your Office files from any device. Whether you're on a computer, tablet, or phone, your work is just a click away. And you don't have to worry about losing anything.

Safe and Secure

OneDrive keeps your Office files safe. It uses strong security measures to protect your work. You can work knowing your files are safe from prying eyes.

Easy to Use

Using OneDrive with Microsoft 365 is easy. It's designed to be user-friendly, so you don't have to be a tech expert to get the hang of it. Just save, share, and go!

Benefits for You

Integrating OneDrive with Microsoft 365 makes your work life easier. You save time, work better with your team, and keep your files safe. It's a smart way to work.

By using OneDrive with Microsoft 365, you're not just saving files but boosting your productivity. Whether it's a big project or a small task, these tools help you do it better.

CHAPTER 9: BACKUP STRATEGIES AND RECOVERY

Now that you've gotten the hang of OneDrive, it's important to note its capability for restoring important files or folders. Begin by opening the OneDrive application. Look for and click on the "Backup" tab, then select "Manage backup." You have the option to back up folders such as Pictures, Desktop, and Documents. Simply choose the files you wish to back up and then click on the "Start backup" button.

AUTOMATIC SYNCING

You should also be familiar with setting up a location on your computer that can automatically sync the files with your OneDrive outline. This will cause it to take all of the files from a particular location on your file and upload them to OneDrive in the manner previously described. You can do this by clicking the "Get the OneDrive applications" link in the screen's bottom left corner. You will click on it, and if you are using Windows 10, you should already have it installed on your computer. However, if you do not already have it installed on your computer, you can go through the download process and install it on your computer. This will also func-tion well on your Mac. Right now, you will click the "Start OneDrive" button, and then you will hit the "Open" button. At this point, all you need to do is enter your address and sign in for it to go through and connect. Your folders in OneDrive will become accessible after you do this. If you click on your OneDrive and simultaneously open up this folder, you will see that the contents stored here are the same ones on your OneDrive, and you will also notice that everything is beginning to sync. Additionally, if you see the green check mark right here, it indicates that it has already been synchronized, which means it is present in both locations, namely on your local computer and in the cloud. If it just shows the cloud, it is only stored in the cloud and has not yet synchronized. However, if it shows a double arrow, it indicates that it is now syncing. You will notice that you have these Clouds if you go down in Windows and look at this section. They may be hiding in your Hidden Icons folder. If you want to view them quickly, you can drag them onto your taskbar. If it is synchronizing, you will notice that it is not blue yet; clicking on it will show you what is occurring. If you choose **"View online**, "youwill just be sent back to the online version of OneDrive.

If you open the folder, anything you save inside will automatically be uploaded to your OneDrive account. So, for instance, if you copy a file from your computer and drop it into your OneDrive Personal, the file will be copied into that location. At that moment, it will say that it is syncing because it is going through, and when that becomes a green check mark, which will show up over your OneDrive Online; therefore, if you refresh it, you will be able to determine whether or not it has synced yet. Keep in mind that whatever you save in the personal folder of your OneDrive will automatically be uploaded to the Online version of your OneDrive, where it will be accessible to you. You can now see that you have several different options available if you right-click on any of the files located in the personal folder of your OneDrive. This is where you can work from the online environment and on your personal computer. When you install this on a computer, it will bring all of your information from your OneDrive. If you install this on three or four different computers, it will sync all of these different ones up, which means that you will have your information living in different places. If this is what you want, then it is fine to do so as long as you have enough space.

Step 1: Sign In to OneDrive

First things first, sign in to your OneDrive account. If you don't have one, creating an account is straightforward. Just go to the OneDrive website and follow the steps.

Step 2: Choose What to Back Up

OneDrive lets you backup your Desktop, Documents, and Pictures folders. To choose, go to the OneDrive settings on your computer. Look for the "Backup" tab and select "Manage backup." Here, you can pick the folders you want to back up.

Step 3: Start the Backup

After selecting your folders, click "Start backup." OneDrive will begin backing up your files. It might take some time, depending on how many files you have.

RECOVERY OPTIONS

The restore options for your files and photos

Microsoft OneDrive Protection and Restoration offers a few ways to recover your files. First, you can restore files from a backup. Second, you can restore files that have suffered unwanted changes. And third, you can restore files that have lost partial data. In ad-dition, OneDrive gives you a detailed log of disk usage activity to see if something abnormal is going on.

Lastly, if you accidentally delete something, you can restore it from your recycling bin. This is where you can find deleted files, photos, or documents. Depending on your settings, restoring a particular file might even be possible. Once you've located your files, click the "Restore" button to restore them.

Once you've restored your files, you can access them on your other devices. To do this, download the OneDrive app from the App Store or Google Play Store. The app will appear on your device's taskbar or bottom-right corner. Next, click on the OneDrive icon. This will take you to the OneDrive Settings page. Finally, select a folder or file to back up.

How To Restore Files

OneDrive 's restoration feature allows you to retrieve lost files for up to 30 days. To help you pinpoint the best moment for file recov-ery, OneDrive offers a histogram that displays the file's activity, guiding you to make an informed decision on when to recover your files. Simply access the file history, choose the files you want to restore, and proceed with any additional options. I. **General Recov-ery (Step by Step)**

When you need to get back to your lost work, OneDrive has your back. Follow these steps to recover or restore your files:

1. **Open OneDrive**: Go to the One Drive website and log in.
2. **Find Lost Files:** Look in your folders for the files you need. If they're not there, check or select the Recycle Bin.
3. **Restore**: Select the files you want and click "Restore" to get them back.

4. After doing that, your file will automatically be restored.

Recovering Deleted Files (Step by Step}

Accidentally deleted something important. No worries. Here's how to bring it back:

1. **Goto the Recycle Bin:** In OneDrive, find the Recycle Bin on the left menu.
2. **Select Your Files:** Click on the files or folders you deleted by mistake.
3. **Restore:** Hit the "Restore" button to put them back where they were.

Recovering Previous Versions (Step by Step)

Made changes to a file and regret it? Retrieve an older version easily:

1. **Right-click the File:** In One Drive, find the file you need an old version of.
2. **Version History:** Choose "Version history" from the menu.
3. **Pick a Version:** You'll see a list of older versions. Pick the one you want.
4. **Restore:** Click "Restore" to replace the current version with the one you chose.

Quick Tips:

- Regularly check your OneDrive setup to make sure it's backing up your important files.

- Use the OneDrive app on your computer or phone for easier access to your files.
- Remember, OneDrive keeps deleted items and old versions for a limited time, so don't wait too long to recover them.

CHAPTER 10: ENHANCING YOUR ONEDRIVE EXPERIENCE

TURNING OFF AUTOMATIC SYNC IN ONEDRIVE

Automatic synchronization is a double-edged sword. While it ensures that your files are always up to date across all devices, it can also consume valuable bandwidth and storage space. Leaming how to manage these settings allows you to synchronize files on your terms, ensuring that only essential data is updated in real-time.

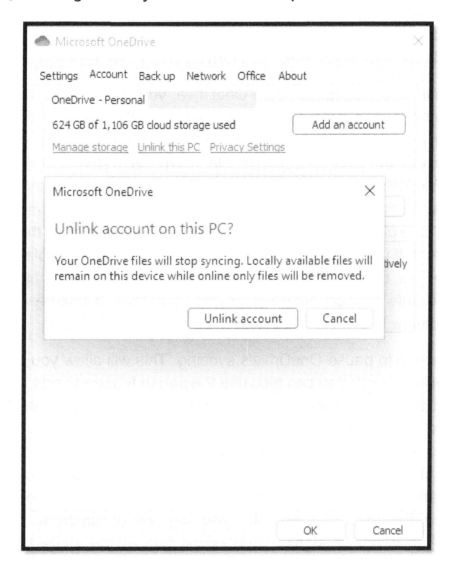

If you've disconnected your computer from your OneDrive account, start by ensuring all desired files are synced to your device. This can be done via the OneDrive tray icons. Navigate to Settings > Account > Choose (Select) folders. Ensure you select the option to syn call files and folders in OneDrive, especially if any were previously unchecked.

This action triggers the download of OneDrive files that are not present on your computer. The process might take some time, but you can monitor progress and estimated completion time by right clicking the OneDrive system tray icon. Once all files are backed up on your computer, right-click the OneDrive system tray icon again and select Settings.

In the Settings tab, uncheck the option "Start OneDrive automatically when I sign in to Windows." Then go to the Account tab and select "Unlink this PC." Promptly click on the "Unlink account" button. This action ceases all syncing activities with your OneDrive account.

What happens if I turn off OneDrive?

Microsoft OneDrive is an integral part of the Microsoft Office suite. However, it can also cause your computer to slow down. Dis-abling the OneDrive application will allow you to free up RAM and CPU, which can be used for other tasks. However, it is essential to note that OneDrive will continue to run when you turn off your PC unless you turn it off yourself.

If you want to unlink your computer from OneDrive, you can do so through the settings tab. There are four options available. The first is to disable syncing. The second option is to unlink your PC from OneDrive completely. This will ensure that your files will no longer be synced with the OneDrive service. OneDrive is a system service that is installed by default on Windows computers. Many users have objected to this inclusion, and disabling it is a simple and permanent solution. It has many advantages but also disad-vantages. One of the main advantages of disabling OneDrive is that your local files will remain in place. If you're concerned about security, you can disable OneDrive using the UAC feature. This option is more secure than the uninstall option. Nevertheless, you should choose a safe method before removing OneDrive. If unsure about the steps, follow the steps below to disable OneDrive.

You can also choose to pause OneDrive's syncing. This will allow you to work on other tasks while OneDrive is off. You can also use the pause feature to edit your files without constantly resyncing. This will also free up your PC's internet bandwidth. Another way to turnoff OneDrive is to unlink your PC and account. This will prevent OneDrive from syncing your files with the cloud. Although you'll still seethe OneDrive icon on your PC's taskbar, it will not sync your files. The next time you login to OneDrive, your files will automatically start syncing again. Another way to stop Microsoft OneDrive is to disable it from starting on Windows. To do this, you can either uncheck "Start OneDrive automatically when Windows signs in "option or disable the entire OneDrive startup process.

To manage your sync preferences, follow these simple steps:

1. **Open OneDrive Settings**: Right-click the OneDrive icon in your system tray and select "Settings."
2. **Adjust Auto Sync:** Go to the "Account" tab and click "Choose folders. " Here, you can select which folders you want automati-cally synced.
3. **Save Your Preferences:** After selecting or deselecting folders, click "OK "to save your changes.

This process helps manage your bandwidth and ensures that only essential files are kept up to date across your devices.

MAKING ONEDRIVE WORK FOR YOU: CUSTOMIZATION TIPS

OneDrive is like a big digital box where you can keep all your important stuff. But did you know you can arrange this box just the way you like? Here's how you can make OneDrive fit just right for the way you work and play.

1. Choose What You See First

When you open OneDrive, you can decide what shows up first. Maybe you want to see your pictures or your school projects. Here's how:

- Open OneDrive online and look for "Settings"(it's usually a little gear icon).
- Click on "Options," and then you'll see a list where you can pick what you see first, like your files or photos.

2. Picking Your Folders

You don't have to keep everything in one big pile. You can choose which folders you want to sync to your computer. This means you can keep some things just in the cloud and some things on your computer, too.

- Right -click the OneDrive icon on your computer (down by the clock).
- Go to "Settings, " then "Account," and click "Choose folders." Now, you can check the boxes for the folders you want on your computer.

3. Making Files Easy to Find

You can change how your files look so it's easier to find what you need. Want a big view or a list? You can decide.

- When you're looking at your files in OneDrive online, find the "View" option (it looks like a little picture).
- Choose how you want to see your files: as big icons, a list, or even pictures.

4. Sharing the Way You Want

Sharing stuff with friends or family? You can set who can see your files and what they can do with them.

- Right -cli ck the file or folder in OneDrive you want to share.
- Choose "Share," and then you can pick if people can edit or just look at your files.

5. Quick Access to What Matters

If you use some files a lot, you can make them easy to find.

- Find the file or folder you use a lot.
- Right -click it and choose "Add to My files" or "Pin to top" if you're online. This way, it's always right there when you open OneDrive.

By setting up OneDrive this way, it's like making your digital space comfy for you. You get to decide what's important and keep your digital stuff just the way you like it. Remember, it's your space, so have fun making it perfect for you!

MAXIMIZING STORAGE SPACE

OneDrive is like a big digital box where you can keep all your important stuff-photos, documents, and more. But just like a real box, it can get full. Here's how to make sure you always have enough space.

Seeing What's Taking Up Space

First off, let's see what's filling up your OneDrive. You can check this by going to the OneDrive website and looking at the bottom left corner. It tells you how much space you've used.

Cleaning Up

Got too much stuff? Time to clean. Go through your files and delete things you don't need anymore. Remember to empty the recycle bin in OneDrive too, or those files will still count against your space.

Saving Space with Photos

Photos can take up a lot of room. If you have lost, think about using the OneDrive photo setting that makes them smaller. They'll still look good, but they won't take up as much space.

Files On-Demand

If you use a computer, there's a cool trick called "Files On -Deman d." It lets you see all your files in OneDrive without having them all on your computer. This way, you save space on your computer and still see everything in OneDrive.

Sharing Instead of Sending

Have a big file you need to give someone? Instead of sending the file directly, share a link to it in OneDrive. This way, you only need one copy, and you don't use up more space.

Keep Only What You Need

Sometimes, we keep old versions of files we don't need. You can set OneDrive to only keep the latest versions of your documents. This saves space because you're not keep in gold stuff you don't look at anymore.

Check Your Plan

Finally, if you're still running out of space, check your OneDrive plan. Maybe it's time fora little more room. You can get more space from OneDrive if you need it.

CHAPTER 11: USEFUL TIPS AND TRICKS

OneDrive is one of the most popular cloud storage services. The program provides a range of helpful tips and tricks.

OneDrive sync client

To avoid OneDrive syncing problems, follow Microsoft 's guidelines for file paths, which limit them to 255 characters. When a file's path is long, it is harder to sync with OneDrive. To fix this, you can rename it to make it shorter. If the problem persists after the above steps, you might not be connected to the correct Windows network or the Microsoft account you're using. To fix this, sign in to your account in Windows Settings. You can then choose which files you'd like to sync. Alternatively, you can let Windows sync your files automatically. Only your main folders are synced by default, but you can designate specific folders when setting up the app. Another tip is to sync files from File Explorer to OneDrive. This will automatically sync your files from the Desktop, My Documents, and Pictures folders. However, you should consult your IT team before enabling this feature, as it can affect your bandwidth usage. It will also create a new folder on your desktop. If you encounter conflicts between files, you can try to resolve them by resetting the OneDrive sync client. If this doesn't help, you can try restarting your router or contacting your service provider to resolve the issue. Otherwise, you may need to reset the settings and set up the OneDrive app again. The OneDrive sync client is very easy to use. The main difference between a standard client and a custom client is the size and number of files that can be synced si-multaneously. OneDrive for Business sync clients can download many files at once, which can use up a lot of bandwidth. To prevent this, you can enable Files On-Deman d to limit the initial bandwidth hit. Known folder moves can also affect network performance. OneDrive sync client has several useful features. One of them is restoring previous versions of files. This can be done by right click-ing any file on OneDrive. Another handy feature is embedding files from OneDrive on a website. Finally, you can also view files in the Recycle Bin.

Sharing files in OneDrive

Microsoft OneDrive lets you share files outside of your organization. You can choose who has access to shared files, set the expi-ration date, and specify other recipients. In addition, you can increase your sharing limit if you need to share more files than the basic OneDrive limit. However, you should remember that OneDrive, including EXE files, does not support certain filetypes. You may also need to validate your account, which you can do through the OneDrive website. When you're ready to share a file or folder, you'll have to sign in to OneDrive. You'll need your work, school, or personal credentials to sign in. Once you've signed in, you'll see a list of all the folders and files in your OneDrive account. You can select multiple items by holding down the Command or Ctrl keys.

Sharing files in OneDrive is very easy and convenient. To share a file or folder, click on its name or click "Share" at the top of the sharing dialog box. The recipient will receive an e-mail link to the file or folder. If you'd like to grant someone editing access, enter their e-mail address in the "Edit" field. You can change the permissions if you've made a mistake when sharing a file. You can also set the expiration date for a file to prevent accidental sharing. Once you've done this, you can access the file with an Internet con-nection from any device. If you're unsure how to share files in OneDrive, you can ask the file owner to remove them. You can share files and folders in OneDrive with different people. You can also create links for forwarding. You can also create folders for different purposes. If you're looking for a simple way to share your files with co-workers, OneDrive is a great option. OneDrive also provides high security, so you can keep your data safe. When you share a file or folder, you should choose the "share" or "private" option in OneDrive's sharing dialog box. Then, you can change the permissions for the files or folders by clicking "Manage Access" on the Share dialogue box.

Managing security groups in OneDrive

Managing security groups is a helpful way to control access to OneDrive. Depending on your organization's needs, you can create different groups for different roles and people. For example, you can create a security group for new employees, legal review team members, vendors, and alliance partners. By defining different security groups, you can automatically protect certain content and prevent access by anonymous users. Once you've created security groups, you can manage their membership. Click the "Members " tab and click the "Manage Members" option. This will display all security group members and allow you to add or remove them.

You can also add resources to each security group. Groups are also useful for managing access to SharePoint sites. Security groups are easy to create and maintain. The group users with similar permissions so that you can assign access to them once. To create a security group, visit the admin center in Office 365. You can also assign users to a security group in SharePoint. OneDrive security groups allow administrators to restrict access to data from specific locations. Using location-based policies will ensure that only trusted devices have access to data. You can also set up multi-factor authentication for workers and guests. Microsoft Endpoint Manager (Microsoft's endpoint management tool) is an excellent choice for organizations concerned about unauthorized access to company data. Using this software, admins can take stock of their entire endpoint environment, including bring-your-own- device scenarios, and take appropriate action to prevent data breaches. One of the most common OneDrive security threats is human error. Users make mistakes and share their files with the wrong accounts. This can lead to data loss, unwanted changes, or malware infections. When using Microsoft OneDrive, you should use complex passwords and password protection to ensure your data remains safe. Security groups in SharePoint are a great way to control access and permissions. By using security groups, ad-ministrators can manage group members centrally. In addition to SharePoint sites, security groups can control access to files on file shares, SharePoint lists, and more. Groups are also helpful for e-mail distribution. In addition, security groups eliminate the need to manage individual users. SharePoint groups automatically remove members when they leave the security groups.

Protecting every version of a file

When it comes to protecting your files on Microsoft OneDrive, there are several things you can do to help keep them safe. Using two-factor verification, which requires an extra security code when you sign in, is a great option. This way, you can be sure that your files will not be accessed by anyone else. OneDrive also recommends encrypting your files when you store them on your mo-bile device. As a result, your files will remain safe even if you lose or steal your device. Microsoft OneDrive supports version history for all file types. You can create a different version for each if you have more than one file. This will give you a greater chance of protecting your files from ransomware. It will also help if you need to recover your files in case of accidental deletion or corruption.

Using version history also gives you the advantage of easily recovering old files. Another option is to redirect known folders back to your PC. For instance, you can protect the Temporary Internet Files folder so people cannot edit your file. That way, only people with the right permissions can edit the document. However, if you trust the folder's contents, you can allow them to edit the document.

CHAPTER 12: SOLVING COMMON PROBLEMS

OneDrive users who experience problems with their storage space may need to free up some space by deleting old files, using an external hard drive, or shrinking the file size using compression tools. It is also important to wait until automatic sync is started before deleting old files. OneDrive users utilizing an organization's server may also encounter problems. In this case, users must contact their IT departments for assistance.

File paths should be shorter

One of the biggest problems with Microsoft OneDrive is that file paths aren't always short enough. Long file paths can cause your OneDrive account to crash. Luckily, there are several ways to make file paths shorter. You can start by renaming your files. This will shorten them to a single letter.

Having a long file path can also prevent your OneDrive files from syncing. To fix this problem, you can rename or move the target file in OneDrive or shorten its file path. You should also avoid having too many subfolders in your OneDrive account and file types that are not supported.

Another way to shorten file paths is to follow Microsoft 's documentation on naming files, paths, and namespaces. You can also use the subset command to shorten file paths. This can help prevent files from exceeding 255 characters, the maximum length for a file name in Windows. OneDrive users often complain about long folder names. Long folder names make it difficult to copy or backup files. Therefore, it's a good idea to change the Organization name in OneDrive to shorten the folder name. To change the Organiza-tion name, you can go into the Settings menu and click on the Account tab. Then, you should change the name of your organization to another one.

Internet connection speed affects synchronization

If you've had trouble synchronizing your OneDrive account with your other devices, you may have an issue with your Internet connection. Microsoft OneDrive is deeply integrated into the Windows ecosystem, and signing in is essential when you first use the service. If you're not signed in, the OneDrive icon in your Windows taskbar will be greyed out. To sign in, click on the OneDrive icon and enter your e-mail address.

If your Internet connection speed is slow, you may experience problems with OneDrive synchronization. First, ensure your Internet connection speed is high enough to transfer large files. If you're unsure whether your Internet connection is fast enough, ping Mi-crosoft's servers. This will give you an idea of how much your Internet connection can transfer. If your connection is slow, you can temporarily pause the synchronization process. If it still takes too long to sync, you can restart your PC.

Lastly, don't attempt to synchronize too many files or folders simultaneously. If you do, you may pause the syncing process if you need to move or delete files. You can also check your Internet connection speed by checking your upload and download rates. For example, when synchronizing OneDrive, you can pause syncing if you experience slow upload or download rates. Then, try to un- link the OneDrive account that is causing problems. To unlink your OneDrive account, you will need to sign in again. You can search for solutions on the Micros oft forums if that doesn't work. Alternatively, you can always try contacting your service provider.

Another thing you should check is your CPU usage. OneDrive will use CPU and RAM when it synchronizes data, so if your internet connection is slow, it can slow down your computer. By opening the Task Manager, you can also check how much of your com-puter's resources OneDrive uses. If this does not work, you can move problematic documents outside the syncing folder and restart syncing. In addition, if the files sync slowly, you may have a bandwidth throttle set upon your account. To turn off this option, open the OneDrive settings window. Another way to improve OneDrive synchronization is to delete the files causing the issue. You can also unlink your PC and account from OneDrive. This way, you can still use OneDrive by saving files locally. However, this can be a painful experience, so you should investigate your options before trying anything else.

Resetting OneDrive fixes problems

If your OneDrive account isn't syncing correctly, you can reset it by choosing the "Unlink this PC" link in the "Account" tab. Once you've done this, you should see the OneDrive icon again. If you don't see it, click "Add an account." Then, follow the instructions to synchronize your data. You may have to resync manually if you have multiple files in OneDrive or have large files to sync. First, you need to check the OneDrive app. Ensure you're running the latest Windows update if it's not running. If that doesn't solve the issue, restart the program. The OneDrive app should appear again after a few minutes. You can also try re-establishing the connection by pressing the Windows + R keys. You may need to update your OneDrive account manually if it doesn't. Once the OneDrive app is back up and running, you can try using Mobile Trans - Back-up by Wonder share. OneDrive users often experience problems with synchronizing their files. To resolve this, ensure your files do not exceed 100GB for personal accounts and 15GB for work or school accounts. You can also try zipping your files to synchronize them. Finally, you can check if any of your files have been accidentally saved, moved, or deleted. If you can't log into OneDrive, check your internet connection first. OneDrive will send you an alert if it can't connect. Then, restart your router or contact your service provider if the problem persists. Finally, if you are still experiencing problems, you should periodically check OneDrive to see if the problem is fixed. If you cannot synchronize your files with OneDrive because of a poor internet connection, restarting the OneDrive app may solve the issue.

In addition, restarting Windows is another way to fix OneDrive problems. This way, you can restore the original settings and restore synchronization. You can also try installing updates to your computer to prevent recurring problems. If your OneDrive account is frozen, follow the steps in the following article. You should follow the instructions provided by Microsoft to fix frozen accounts. If you can't find any instructions, you can look for help in Microsoft's forums. These forums contain hundreds of posts. Alternatively, you can create a new post and look for information about your problem. Some users report problems synchronizing OneDrive files after updating their OS. This can be due to large files or a bad connection. In this case, it's recommended to rename files using shorter file names. Renaming folders on the OneDrive directory to be shorter than the original name will ensure that the file paths are shorter.

The troubleshooting app will ask you to enter your Admin password to begin the scan. First, ensure that your computer is connected to the internet to connect to the Microsoft servers. Otherwise, the troubleshooting app won't work correctly. If the trou-ble shooting process fails, it is likely that your OneDrive is not connected to the internet.

Diagnostic Tools

When something goes wrong with OneDrive, figuring out the problem is important. This section will show you how to use some tools and resources to find and fix issues with your OneDrive.

Step1: Check the OneDrive Status

First, see if OneDrive is running correctly. Look for the OneDrive icon on your computer. If it's not happy (like showing a red X or a warning sign), there might be a problem.

Step 2: Use the OneDrive Troubleshooter

Windows has a special tool to help fix OneDrive problems. It's called the OneDrive Troubleshooter. You can download it from the Microsoft website. Once you have it, open the tool, and it will try to find and fix any issues.

Step 3: Check Your Internet Connection

Sometimes, the problem is not with OneDrive but with your internet. Make sure your computer is connected to the internet. You can try opening a website to see if your internet is working.

Step 4: Restart OneDrive

If OneDrive is acting up, try restarting it. Right -click the OneDrive icon and choose "Close OneDrive." Then, open OneDrive again and see if that helps.

Step 5: Update OneDrive

Make sure your OneDrive is up to date. If it's not, it might not work right. You can update OneDrive through the Microsoft Store or the OneDrive website.

Step 6: Contact Support

If you've tried everything and OneDrive still isn't working, it might be time to ask for help. You can contact Microsoft support for more assistance. They can help figure out what's wrong and how to fix it.

SUMMARY OF COMMON PROBLEMS AND SOLUTIONS IN ONEDRIVE

OneDrive is a great tool, but sometimes you might run into problems. Here are solutions to some common issues.

Problem 1: Can't Sign In

Solution: Check your internet connection first. Then, make sure your login details are correct. If you still can't sign in, reset your password.

Problem 2: Files Not Syncing

Solution: Make sure you're connected to the internet. Then, check if the file size is within the OneDrive limits. Restarting OneDrive can also help.

Problem 3: Lost or Deleted Files

Solution: Go to the OneDrive website and check the Recycle Bin. You can restore files from there. If it's not there, you might need to contact support.

Problem 4: OneDrive Is Full

Solution: Delete files you don't need from OneDrive or buy more storage. You can also move files to a different storage space.

Problem 5: File Version Issues

Solution: Use the version history feature on the OneDrive website to restore an earlier version of the file.

Problem 6: Sharing Issues

Solution: Check the sharing settings for the file or folder. Make sure the person you're sharing with has the correct permissions.

Problem 7: Slow Sync Speed

Solution: This can happen if your internet is slow or if you're syncing a lot of files at once. Pause and resume syncing or try syncing fewer files at a time.

Problem 8: Installation Problems

Solution: Make sure your device meets the system requirements for OneDrive. You might need to update your operating system or reinstall OneDrive.

CONTACTING SUPPORT

Step 1: Identify the Issue

Before reaching out for support, clearly identify the problem you're experiencing. Try to pinpoint what's not working or what error messages you're seeing. This will help you explain your issue more clearly and find a solution faster.

Step2: Use Built-in Help

OneDrive has a built-in help feature. You can access it directly from the app or web interface. Look for the "Help" option or a ques-tion mark icon. Typing in your issue here can provide you with instant solutions or guide you through troubleshooting steps.

Step 3: Visit the OneDrive Support Page

Microsoft has a comprehensive support page for OneDrive. It includes articles, guides, and troubleshooting tips for common prob-lems. Visit this page and use the search function to find information about your specific issue.

Step 4: Use the Microsoft Community

The Microsoft Community is a great resource where you can post your issue and get answers from other OneDrive users and ex-perts. Often, someone else has had the same problem, and you can find solutions by searching the community posts.

Step 5: Contact Support Directly

If you can't solve your issue with the steps above, you can contact Microsoft support directly. You can do this through the OneDrive app by going to the "Help & Settings" menu and selecting "Email OneDrive support." If you're using OneDrive on the web, scroll to the bottom of the page and click on "Contact Support."

Step 6: Prepare Your Details

Before contacting support, gather all necessary details about your issue. This includes your device type, operating system, OneDrive version, and any error messages you're receiving. Having this information ready will make the support process smoother.

Step 7: Follow Instructions Carefully

Once you've contacted support, make sure to follow any instructions given carefully. Support may provide you with steps to trou-ble shoot your issue or request further information. Following their guidance accurately will help resolve your issue more quickly.

Step 8: Feedback

After your issue is resolved, you might receive a feedback survey. Taking the time to fill this out can help improve the support expe-rience for you and others in the future.

CHAPTER 13: PRACTICAL APPLICATIONS

OneDrive helps students save their school projects online. This way, they don't lose their work if their computer breaks. They can also work on their projects from any computer, not just their own. Families use OneDrive to share photos and videos. They create folders for vacations or birthdays and invite family members to add their own photos. This keeps memories safe and easy to find. Writers store their manuscripts on OneDrive. They can access their work from anywhere, making it easy to write whenever inspi-ration strikes. They also share documents with editors for real-time feedback. Small businesses rely on OneDrive for keeping important files. Contracts, invoices, and client information are stored securely. This makes it easy to find what they need, fast. Teachers share educational materials with students through OneDrive. They upload reading materials, assignments, and videos. Students access these from home, making learning flexible. Photographers' backup their photos to OneDrive. They create organized folders for each photoshoot. This protects their work and makes it easy to share with clients. Non-profit s coordinate projects using OneDrive. They plan events, track donations, and share reports. Everyone stays informed and can contribute no matter where they are. Travelers keep copies of their important documents in OneDrive. Passports, tickets, and itineraries are safe and accessible. This reduces stress during travel. Fitness trainers upload workout plans and diet charts for their clients. They track progress and make updates in real-time. This personalized approach helps clients achieve their goals. Researchers collaborate on studies using OneDrive. They share data and findings securely. These speeds up their work and helps in making new discoveries. Freelancers manage their portfolios with OneDrive. They show their work to potential clients easily. This helps them get more projects. Event planners organize details of events on OneDrive. Guest lists, venue contracts, and schedules are all in one place. They can also share plans with clients for feedback. Musicians store their music files and sheet music in OneDrive. Bands can work on songs together, even when they're apart. They also share their music with producers or fans. Real estate agents keep property listings and client details on OneDrive. They access information quickly during meetings with clients. This helps them provide better service. Volun-teers coordinate relief efforts using OneDrive. They share information about what's needed and were. This makes their help more effective.

CONCLUSION

As we conclude our journey through the "Microsoft OneDrive Guide 2024 for Beginners," it is essential to reflect on the comprehensive and transformative potential that OneDrive brings to its users. This guide has been meticulously designed to provide a thorough understanding of OneDrive, from its basic functionalities to its advanced features, offering you the tools and knowledge necessary to leverage this powerful platform effectively. Whether you are a novice or looking to deepen your expertise, this book aims to empower you with the skills needed to navigate the digital landscape confidently.

Embracing the Cloud Revolution

The transition to cloud storage represents a significant shift in how we manage, access, and share our digital content. OneDrive stands at the forefront of this revolution, offering a seamless and integrated solution that addresses the evolving needs of users. By embracing OneDrive, you are not merely adopting a new tool; you are participating in a broader movement towards more efficient, secure, and collaborative ways of working and living.

Throughout this guide, we have explored the fundamental aspects of OneDrive, starting with its history and development. Understanding the evolution of OneDrive provides valuable context, highlighting Microsoft's commitment to continuous improvement and innovation. This historical perspective sets the stage for appreciating the robust features and capabilities that OneDrive offers today.

Key Takeaways

One of the critical aspects of OneDrive is its integration within the Microsoft ecosystem. This integration is not just about convenience; it represents a strategic advantage that enhances productivity and collaboration. OneDrive's seamless compatibility with Microsoft Office applications, Teams, SharePoint, and Outlook creates a unified environment where users can effortlessly move between tasks and projects. This interconnectedness simplifies workflows, reduces redundancy, and ensures that your digital tools work together harmoniously.

Accessibility is another cornerstone of OneDrive. In a world where mobility and flexibility are paramount, OneDrive ensures that your files are always within reach, regardless of your location or device. This ubiquitous access is facilitated by OneDrive's cross-platform compatibility, enabling you to sync and access your files from desktops, laptops, tablets, and smartphones. This level of accessibility empowers you to stay productive and connected, whether you are working from home, traveling, or collaborating with remote teams.

Security and Trust

Security is a paramount concern in the digital age, and OneDrive addresses this with robust measures designed to protect your data. From encryption to two-step verification and ransomware detection, OneDrive provides multiple layers of security to safeguard your files. The Personal Vault feature adds an extra layer of protection for sensitive documents, ensuring that your most critical data remains secure.

For businesses and enterprises, OneDrive for Business offers advanced security and compliance features. These tools are essential for organizations that must adhere to strict regulatory standards and protect sensitive information. By providing a secure environment for data storage and collaboration, OneDrive for Business supports the operational needs of companies while ensuring that data integrity and security are maintained.

Collaboration and Productivity

Collaboration is at the heart of modern workflows, and OneDrive excels in facilitating effective teamwork. The real-time co-authoring feature allows multiple users to work on the same document simultaneously, fostering collaboration and reducing the time spent on back-and-forth revisions. This capability is particularly valuable for teams working on projects, as it enables seamless integration and communication.

OneDrive's collaboration tools extend beyond document editing. The ability to share files and folders with specific individuals or groups, set permissions, and track changes ensures that your collaborative efforts are well-coordinated and efficient. These features make OneDrive an indispensable tool for project management, remote work, and any scenario where teamwork is essential.

Advanced Features and Customization

OneDrive is not just a storage solution; it is a versatile platform with a range of advanced features that cater to diverse needs. Throughout this guide, we have explored these features, from file management and synchronization to backup and recovery strategies. These capabilities allow you to customize OneDrive to suit your specific requirements, whether you are an individual user, a student, or a business professional.

The advanced features of OneDrive also include powerful search functionalities, which leverage artificial intelligence to help you find files quickly and accurately. This intelligent search capability enhances your productivity by reducing the time spent searching for documents and ensuring that you can locate critical information when needed.

The Future of OneDrive

Looking ahead, the future of OneDrive is filled with exciting possibilities. As technology continues to evolve, OneDrive is poised to incorporate new advancements that will further enhance its functionality and user experience. The integration of artificial intelligence and machine learning, for example, promises to bring even more intelligent features, such as automated organization, predictive file management, and personalized recommendations.

OneDrive's commitment to sustainability and green technology is another area of future growth. By investing in energy-efficient data centers and eco-friendly practices, Microsoft is ensuring that OneDrive not only meets the needs of its users but also contributes positively to the environment. This commitment aligns with broader global efforts to create more sustainable and responsible technological solutions.

Practical Applications and Real-World Impact

Throughout this guide, we have highlighted various practical applications of OneDrive, demonstrating how it can be used effectively in different contexts. From personal file storage and academic projects to business operations and enterprise-level collaboration, OneDrive offers solutions that address a wide range of needs.

The real-world impact of OneDrive is evident in its ability to streamline workflows, enhance productivity, and improve data security. By adopting OneDrive, users can simplify their digital lives, reduce the risk of data loss, and create more efficient and collaborative working environments. These benefits translate into tangible improvements in both personal and professional spheres, making OneDrive a valuable tool for anyone looking to optimize their use of cloud storage.

Final Thoughts

As we conclude this guide, it is important to recognize that the journey with OneDrive does not end here. The principles, practices, and insights shared in this book are meant to be a starting point for your ongoing exploration and mastery of OneDrive. The digital landscape is constantly evolving, and staying updated with the latest tools and technologies is essential for maintaining a competitive edge.

OneDrive offers a dynamic and flexible platform that can adapt to your changing needs. Whether you are managing personal files, collaborating with a team, or running a business, OneDrive provides the tools and features necessary to achieve your goals. By adopting the OneDrive mindset, you are positioning yourself to take full advantage of the opportunities that cloud storage offers.

In conclusion, the "Microsoft OneDrive Guide 2024 for Beginners" has been designed to equip you with the knowledge and skills needed to make the most of OneDrive. From understanding its basic functionalities to exploring advanced features, this guide has provided a comprehensive overview of what OneDrive can do. As you continue to use and explore OneDrive, remember that the key to success lies in embracing the principles of accessibility, collaboration, security, and continuous learning.

Thank you for embarking on this journey with us. We hope that this guide has been informative, engaging, and empowering. As you move forward, we encourage you to continue exploring the capabilities of OneDrive, staying curious, and seeking out new ways to enhance your digital experience. The future is bright with OneDrive, and we are excited to see how you will use this powerful tool to achieve your goals and transform your digital life.

Made in the USA
Monee, IL
21 December 2024

74938517R00063